On the Cover
Like the Christian cross or the American flag, the teepee became an iconic symbol. It represents the Plains American Indians, like the tomahawk and the arrowhead. When viewed, teepees remind us of that time in past history.

(Courtesy of Azusa Publishing, LLC)

Parts of this text have been taken from the author's previous book as a revision to convey the history of the tribes described, so as not to lose the necessary content.

AMERICAN INDIAN TRIBES OF IDAHO

Robert David Bolen, B.A.

Robert W. Butler

Dedication
Page
I dedicate this work to my wife Dori, my sons Jeromy,
Jim and Ryan and my daughters, Brooke and Kerri.

PHOTOS, MAPS AND DRAWINGS

Page #   Pag

CONTENTS
AMERICAN INDIAN TRIBES OF IDAHO

Acknowledgements

I would like to extend a very special thank you to the Azusa ublishing, LLC, for the excellent pictures copied into my previous ook, "Smoke Signals & Wagon Tracks" and for the photos used in this xt. Many customers point to the photos in the book and remark how uch they enjoy them. Theresa has the most excellent postcards, with hotos of Indians and the Old West for your own research or enjoyment. heck them out on the net at Azusapublishing.com!

Thank you to my wife, Dori, for all of your help. I want to thank ed Eddins, author of "Mountains of Stone," for great photos! I want to xpress my gratitude to George and Lise' Jumper for the Appaloosa pix. would like to express my appreciation to Allen Frank Owen and Sonia 1artin for their editing. Thanks a lot to the staff of the Idaho Historical ociety Library for your photo assistance in this work and to the Idaho tate Historical Museum for pix of Sacajawea. Thank you to the Nevada listorical Society for the pictures of Sarah and Old Chief Winnemucca. I ant to thank the Library of Congress for the excellent wickiup photo nd the Smithsonian Institute for the rare photo of Washakie's village. I ould like to say thank you to Len Sodenkamp for the unique artist's ndition of "Old Fort Boise," Fort Hall and the Bannock Indian ketches. Hat's off to the Wal-Mart Photo staff for their countless hours f processing pictures. Last, but not least, my sincerest thanks to Fed-Ex ffice for their great job of cover work, aligning the picture order and rinting this publication.

#1. Plains Indian Woman, Horse and Travois- Teepees were collapse folded and hauled on two poles, drug behind a horse, called a travois. Teepe skins, goods and infants were hauled on the devise. With additional poles, teepee was erected. Prior to the horse, goods were hauled, using a small travois by domestic dogs.

(Photograph Courtesy of Azusa Publishing, LLC)

FOREWORD

The "American Indian Tribes of Idaho," is a history of the aboriginal people of Northwestern America. Native Americans call themselves "the first people." When Europeans arrived in America they called the natives, "Indians," because their facial features and skin color resembled the natives of East India. The name, Indians carried over and the term is still in use. Indians refer to themselves as "the people," in their own language. Theories are that the Aboriginal Indian came across the Bering Straits corridor from Siberia in waves, after the Ice Age, perhaps around 15,000 years B.P. It is speculated that approximately 13,000 years B.P. early man dwelled on American shores. Evidence of Clovis man was found from Alaska to Mexico and throughout America. He used the atlatl sling to thrust five foot darts into the Woolly Mammoth, Bison-bison, Giant Sloth, camel and other large beasts for food. The plains of Northwest America teemed in herds of antelope, bison, deer and elk, as well as smaller mammals and birds. The semi-arid high desert region of the Great Basin and the mountainous Plateau in the North became inhabited by seven American Indian tribes. The Northern Plateau region contained numerous 10,000 foot mountain ranges, including the Bitterroots and Tetons. On the east lies the Continental Divide. River drainages and creeks provided natural resources for inhabitation by various tribes of Indians. The land now known as Idaho contained 83,557 square miles, rich in game, water and trees.

Seven tribes of American Indians were indigenous to this territory. The Bannock, Northern Paiute, and Northern Shoshoni Indians were the southern tribes in the region that became Idaho. Coeur d'Alene, Kalispel, Kutenai and Nez Perce Indians were the northern tribes living in the Plateau region. Of seven tribes there were four distinct language groups: the Kutenai, Sahaptian, Salish and Uto-Aztecan (Shoshonean-Aztecan) stock. The Coeur d'Alene and Kalispel (Pend d'Oreille) were from the Salish speaking group. The Kutenai language stood alone. The Sahaptian was the Nez Perce language and included the Umatilla and Yakima Indian speakers. The Bannock, N. Paiute and Shoshoni were all Uto-Aztecan speakers of the Numic division called the Paviotso (Bannock and N. Paiute dialects) and the Shoshone (the Shoshoni dialects). The Blackfoot, Palouse and Spokane Indians roamed this country but were not sedentary..

These Indians arrived approximately 3,000 years B.P. and have dwelled on the land in North America as "Hunters and Gathers," the nomadic tribes came to hunt the region rich in game. When the American Indian found a geographic area of prosperity he became more sedentary. The men made weapons for hunting to attain meat and brought home game which was shared with the extended family. The women gathered nuts, seeds and berries. They foraged for food, caught small rodents, and insects. Indian women dug an assortment of edible roots from the ground to provide sustenance. The Camas root was their favorite. Camas root was pounded in mortar and pestles, to bake bread. Women had wife duties, and the children.

Indians showed no ownership of the land they were territorial and did not want enemy Indians on their borders. The young warrior learned to count coup, a game of war to surprise the enemy, run or ride up and get in his face. He would then strike him with a quirt as a sign of bravery. This progressed to combat in warfare. In Historic times scalping was learned from the French. The warrior would remove a circle of scalp and hair from his foe as a trophy.

Only the Norseman and the Spanish Conquistadors had arrived on the continent, until the Lewis and Clark, in 1804. They opened the Northwest for passage, befriending the Indian, traveling through Idaho, 200 years ago. The Hudson's Bay Fur Trading Company expanded into America from Canada setting up the Fur Trade with the Indians. Fur forts were built and the mountain men arrived, married Indians and lived with them, while trapping furs.

As Euro-Americans arrived in covered wagons, many Indians were friendly, others attacked. Some emigrants shot Indians. Indians first raided. At times they massacred everyone on the wagon-train. Fear of Indian attacks spread among the emigrants. Indians Wars broke out and President Abraham Lincoln transferred Union soldiers from the Civil War to the Western front to protect the people. Military posts were established. Indian Wars were fought with various tribes. At the end, the Indians were defeated. White man brought deadly diseases west that greatly reduced Indian populations. With the combination of war, disease and the removal of the buffalo, the American Indians numbers were greatly reduced. Indians were ordered onto government reservations and the fighting was ended.

#2. Map of Idaho
Indian Tribes (Author Photo)

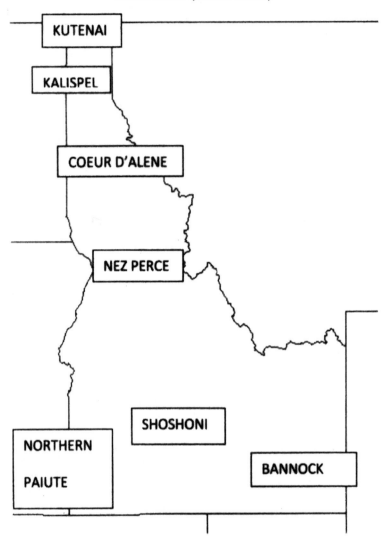

KUTENAI

KALISPEL

COEUR D'ALENE

NEZ PERCE

SHOSHONI

NORTHERN

PAIUTE

BANNOCK

Chapter One
SHOSHONI INDIANS

The Northern Shoshoni (Shoshone) Indians call themselves, "Newe" or the people. When the white men saw the Bannock, Paiute and Shoshoni women digging roots, they called them "Digger Indians." When the Shoshoni obtained horses, they were referred to as "Horse-mounted Shoshoni." Shoshoni bands without horses were called "Walking Indians," by their peers. Nearby Indian tribes spoke of them, using sign language, making a slithering hand motion, as snake, to demonstrate how the Shoshoni Indians vanished behind rocks.' They were classified as "Plains Indians," because they were "Hunters of the Buffalo."

The Bannock, Paiute and Shoshoni tribes spoke similar dialects of the Shoshonean or Uto-Aztecan language family, as Numic speakers. Shoshonean is a widespread language family that ranged mainly over California, Idaho, W. Oregon, Nevada, N. Utah, and W. Wyoming. Hopi Indians in Arizona, Ute Indians in Colorado, and the Aztec Indians in Mexico were of the Uto-Aztecan language family. No written language existed in the beginning. Indians carved elaborate petro-glyphs in caves, on rock walls, boulders and flat stones. Some believe this to be only a form of "rock art." Instead, maps, historic accounts and murals are etched in rock depicting events, recorded in time. Messages on bark were left along the trail for others. The various tribes used a universal "sign language" to communicate, when there was no interpreter.

This country had been carefully chosen by ancestral Shoshoni. The climate was relatively mild except in intense summer heat and heavy snowfall. The natural resources of these regions were rich with flora and fauna. The land teemed with animals in a variety of fish, game and flora to comfortably sustain them. It became central Idaho in the northern Great Basin cultural region. The Northern Plateau is mountainous with woodlands, lakes and rivers, with increased precipitation. Trees grew above the tree line of the Rocky Mountains and along rivers. The Salmon River drains into the Middle Snake River.

In the Northern Plateau, the Salmon River bands were referred to as the Salmon-eater Shoshoni or "Agai-deka," by their peers. These Indians intermixed, marrying neighboring Paiute, Shoshoni and even Nez Perce Indians. With the Salmon River's four large tributaries and yearly salmon runs, the beautiful Plateau region was a Mecca for inhabitance. Fish made up over half of the Salmon-eaters diet. They caught bull trout, Chinook salmon, cutthroat trout, mountain whitefish, rainbow trout, and steelhead in the Salmon River. Mountain lakes held land-locked kokanee salmon. Wild bear, deer and elk roamed free. Canadian geese were plentiful. Hares and other mammals were in access and the timbers teemed in game.

The Sheep-eater Shoshoni lived in the Plateau region farther north in the Upper Snake and Salmon River Country of the Northern Rockies on into Yellowstone. They were called "Tukudekas," by their peers. Shoshoni that lived in this region learned to adapt to the semi-arid high desert terrain with its sparse vegetation. The Sheep-eater Shoshoni were considered the most skilled Indian hunters. They became expert in hunting elusive mountain sheep in the Rocky Mountain heights. The Sheep-eaters made fine bow and arrows. Their bows were crafted from the horns (rack) of the mountain sheep. They used domestic dogs to pull travois and haul their goods. Their shelters were caves or temporary skin huts. Mormon missionaries named the Salmon-eater and the Sheep-eater Shoshoni, Lemhi Shoshoni. They were "Walking Shoshoni."

In prehistoric times, the Bannock, an offshoot of the Northern Paiute, migrated into the region near the Fort Hall Shoshoni. Eventually the Shoshoni and Paiute intermarried. Over time they became one tribe, the Shoshoni-Bannock people. The romance between the two tribes continues, today. Fort Hall Shoshoni dwelled in the Snake River bottoms around the Fort Hall Fur Trading Post. They caught the Yellowstone cutthroat and rainbow trout in the nearby creeks.

Bear River Shoshoni are Northern Shoshoni that lived in eastern Idaho Territory along Bear Lake and the Bear River drainage in the southeastern corner of what is now Idaho. They caught cutthroat and rainbow trout and mountain whitefish in the Bear River.

The Northern Paiute lived west of the Shoshoni in what is now Oregon and Nevada before migrating north into the western river drainages of now Idaho. The headwaters of the Boise River begin in the Sawtooth Mountains, flow across Idaho and empty into the Snake and Columbia Rivers into the Pacific Ocean.

The Boise, Payette and Weiser Rivers flow into the upper Snake River. The Northern Shoshoni Indians were named for the Snake River drainages where they dwelled. They were the Boise, Bruneau and the Weiser River Shoshoni. The bands lived in close proximity with a socio-political alliance between them, including marriage. Over time the Boise and Bruneau River Shoshoni inter-married so often that they became one people. The Army called them and the Sheep-eater Shoshoni the Western Shoshoni. The Boise River basin was the favorite haunt of the Boise River Shoshoni, who dwelled at the mouth of the Boise River, where it empties into the mighty Snake River in a peaceful valley, under cottonwood trees, where the weather was mild. Horses grazed on the Boise River bottoms. Here the Snake River formed the western boundary of Idaho Territory. Buffalo, fish, roots, salmon and wild vegetables were the main staples in their diet. The Boise River teemed with Chinook salmon, bull, cutthroat, and rainbow trout with mountain whitefish. Salmon swam up river to spawn in the Boise River until 1860, when the phenomena ended. They fished the Boise River from the salmon run in the spring into autumn. The Salmon Festival was followed by the Shoshoni Trade Fair, at the mouth of the Boise River. The Weiser River Band of Shoshoni Indians evolved from a northern mountain band of Sheep-eater, who intermarried with Bannock and Nez Perce. The Weiser band fished for mountain white fish, salmon, bull and rainbow trout in the Weiser River and dwelled in Indian Valley. Fish made up much of their diet. The Bruneau River Shoshoni dwelled on the Bruneau

iver drainage. They depended on fish, groundhog, pine nuts, roots, and seeds
nd caught bull trout, rainbow trout and mountain whitefish in the Bruneau
iver. Their peers called them Groundhog-eaters ("Yahan-deka"). The Bruneau
hoshoni moved south to harvest pine nuts. During autumn they moved up onto
e Camas Prairie to dig the Camas roots.

BANDS

The Shoshoni bands were composed of an extended family or a composite
and. A composite band could have been unrelated. Three or four generations of one
mily normally lived and traveled in one small band and had no headman. They had
olitical ties through kinship and dwelled in small camps. These bands seldom
umbered over 30. The Shoshoni, however, did not have societal clans like the wolf
an.

The Snake Indians husband's extended family lived in the territory of the
ibe of his father. Power and property passed down through the father's line. The
hoshoni practiced arraigned marriages. Many tribes practiced polygamy, the act of
aving more than one husband or wife. A man marrying an Indian bride would also
ke her younger sisters for wives; all dwelt in the same lodge. Non-related wives
ad to live in other lodges. If a woman wanted more than one husband, she could
arry her husband's younger brother. The word chief was introduced by the white
an. The Indians had no terminology for chief. Instead, they had a headman, who
ight have been the hunt leader or war leader. Indian agents picked one man as
ief to represent the tribe. Family bands combined in a village or winter camp
ight have had a headman or band chief, social director of ceremonies, dances,
stivals, hunts and war.

The social director was over the dance. The whole village participated in
ancing. The Shoshoni Indians loved music and the dance. Musical instruments used
ere the drums, flutes, mariachis, rattles and whistles. Rattles were made from
ourds, hooves, sewn rawhide (with rocks or animal teeth inside), shells and turtle
ell. Wooden flutes were made from cedar, cherry and walnut wood, Sometimes an
r stop was fashioned into a bird or animal of stone to change the flute pitch.
Vhistles were fashioned from hollow bird bones. The Shoshoni performed the Back
d Forth Dance, Round Dance, Scalp Dance and the War Dance. The Scalp Dance
as done mostly by women dancing around a scalp pole as the men drummed and
layed wooden rasps. The Cry Dance was done in mourning for a loved one who
ad died. The Rain Dance and Warm Dance were executed relating to the weather.
hey formed a huge circle surrounding the camp and dance all night in a vigil to
olift their spirits. Meantime, the medicine man prayed for spiritual cleansing. Night
ongs were sung as prayers for healing the sick. A Pine Nut Dance celebration was
eld the over a three-night period before harvesting pine nuts.

#3. Washakie, Chief of the Green and Wind River Eastern Shoshoni
(Photograph Courtesy of AZUSA PUBLISHING, LLC)

Heebe-Tee-tse, Shoshoni Plains Shoshoni Indian Warrior
(Photograph Courtesy of AZUSA PUBLISHING, LLC)

1

Shoshoni caught young hawks and young eagles in the wild and caged them in stick cages for their feathers which made head-dresses and costumes that were worn in dance celebrations. One feather was given to a young brave when he became a man. Each feather in a headdress stood for an act of bravery or a feat in battle. Shoshoni children had domestic dogs and caught wild animals for pets.

The Shoshoni loved to play games. La Crosse was a favorite game, played with a type of racket and a deerskin ball. Young Shoshoni ran races. Game-pieces were made of bone or stone. The guessing game, of which hand held the game-stone behind the back, was played. Indian boys lagged a piece to the line drawn in the dirt was another game played. One would throw a game-piece while others tossed in an attempt to hit the piece was another game. They played stick games. Young Shoshoni ran foot races.

The Snake Indians loved telling stories, especially in the winter. Mythical tales were told using mythical animated characters explaining creation and life. Indian tales were told of colorful trickster characters, such as Coyote, Star, Rabbit, Arrow Boy and Children of the sun. In the Creation story Coyote created the world with the help of ducks that dove deep down in the water and found plant life. Coyote made people from the mud and made the Earth. Indians young and old loved hearing stories.

A shaman or medicine man led medicine bands who assisted him in warding off evil and healing illness and used magic, charms, fans, fetishes and sometimes peyote (a hallucinatory drug) to perform his feats. The Snake people believed in spirit guides, vision quests and that all things animate or inanimate had life, even the sun, moon and stars, a belief was called animism. The rite-of-passage for a young brave to become a man was the vision quest. He normally ventured out alone into the wild and stayed until he received his vision. Animals and nature were a part of their belief system. He experienced a supernatural vision from nature as an eagle, bear, wolf or magpie spirit, for example. This animal spirit would determine the young brave's spirit guide through life.

INDIAN HOUSES

The Indians found temporary refuge, taking advantage of natural caves, lava tubes, overhangs and rock shelters that made temporary shelters. The Shoshoni built semi-subterranean pit houses (earth lodges) constructed half below ground and half above ground, with earthen walls. The earth provided insulation from the heat and cold. The roof had branches for supports, thatched with rye grass. These houses were relatively small and often crowded for the whole family. The pit house contained a hearth for warmth and cooking their meals inside.

The Plains tipi (teepee) was a large tent. It was constructed over numerous lodge poles in a conical shaped framework, tied near the top. Sinew was used to sew the buffalo skins together. It was covered with skins and anchored at the base with rocks. Matting or hides made the flooring. A teepee took from eight buffalo skins to twenty skins to cover, according to size. They were collapsible for travel. The tent, hides, goods, utilities and infants were hauled this way. The teepee (tipi), was erected quickly with additional lodge-poles.

The wickiup (wigwam) was a cone-shaped hut with upright poles, similar to the tipi. This conical hut was covered with bark, brush, or matting. Rabbit fur blankets kept them warm in the winter plus heated rocks were placed under foot to keep them cozy. The willow hut or thatch hut was similar in construction to the brush hut. Prior to the tipi, a similar dwelling was constructed of long willow poles, tied at the top in a conical configuration. The framework was covered with sewn matting of tule reeds or other thatch material. Brush huts were similar in construction to the wickiup with upright poles tied near the top and sagebrush or branches for covering.

The Shoshoni Indians erected temporary dwellings in the hot desert, called brush huts. They found food in the desert. A shade house was ideal in hot weather. It was constructed with fresh, green sweet smelling birch leaf branches for the roof. It provided much needed cool shade for the Native people. Digging sticks, mortars, winnow baskets and other tools for the harvest were kept there.

Another type of shelter was the longhouse of the northern Lemhi Shoshoni. This dwelling was rectangular, partly underground. Walls were made of saplings lashed together and fastened to uprights. The roof was a woven thatch. The floor was of matting. They contained a hearth for cooking and warmth.

Huts were used for special events. A menstrual hut was one such dwelling. When an Indian girl came of age, she began menstruation. She spent the time of her menses in a hut, called a menstrual hut, isolated on the village perimeter. She would bathe and go through a spiritual cleansing by sprinkling juniper needles, sage or sweet grass on the coals of a fire and draw the smoke toward her (with the motion of her hands), breathing it in. Blood signified her spiritual power. A small ceremony might be held for her rite-of-passage.

Separate huts were used as well for child bearing, also. Time spent in a birthing hut was around 30 days. Shoshoni babies weren't always born in birthing huts. Sometimes the mother would go off into a remote area for privacy to have her child alone. Births were ritualistic and sacred to them. Communal sweat lodges were used by the men to socialize. Sweat baths were followed by a plunge into cold water. The Shoshoni walled up a running hot springs with stones to make a permanent hot tub. The natural spring water contained minerals healthy for the body. The Indians killed deer with bow and arrows. Hunting blinds were constructed in a circle using boulders the size of a basketball or larger. The walls were high enough to conceal the hunters. Remnants of these blinds still exist today in the Northwest.

STONE TOOLS

Native Americans in America were of the stone-age. Lithic tools were made of antler, bone, horn, stone, wood and fastened with sinew. Stone tools were very popular. Arrowheads, awls, fishhooks, gravers, hide scrapers, shaft scrapers, and a host of tools were flint-knapped (chipped) from basalt, chert, or obsidian. Hammers, hand axes, root diggers, shovels and tomahawks were fashioned of larger cores,

Atlatl is an ancient Aztec Indian word for spear thrower. The atlatl was a throwing devise about two foot long with finger-loops on the throwing end and a bone spur on the other to engage the end of the spear. A weight could be added to the underside of the atlatl for momentum. The spear and atlatl were held in one hand. Using the atlatl, the dart (spear) was thrown to increase distance and speed, with extra thrust for 100 yards, to bring down big game, such as the mammoth elephant, giant bison-bison and other large game.

Use of the atlatl transitioned into the age of the bow and arrow, as the size of game decreased. Large game was reduced in size through extinction. The mammoth elephant, the bison-bison and other larger animals were hunted by early man. In time these large creatures died off. The buffalo was the largest land creature hunted by these Indians. After the atlatl came the bow and arrow in the last 2,000 years. The men hunted game with bow and arrows. Fathers taught their sons early, how to use the bow and arrow. The Snake Indians crafted fine bows and arrows of Cedar, Juniper, Oak, Osage and Yew. The bow and arrows they fashioned were admired by other tribes. A shaft was heated and straightened, smoothed and polished for an arrow. Indians flint knapped (chipped) arrowheads from chert or obsidian and inserted them into a slit at the end of the shaft. It was glued with pitch and wrapped with sinew. Bow strings were made from animal gut. Eagle, hawk or similar feathers were used to fletch an arrow.

The Shoshoni were "Hunters and Gathers," as were most American Indians, with division of labor between the sexes. Men hunted and women gathered. Men used bow and arrows to shoot antelope, bear, buffalo, cougar, deer, large birds, moose, mountain sheep, rabbit and other animals for food.

Women foraged for food and gathered berries, fleshy cactus parts, herbs, nuts, roots, seeds. They caught small rodents, gathered insects, lizards and snakes to eat. The practice of eating anything edible sustained them, such as grasshopper, ground squirrel, horned toad, and rattle snake.

Their duties were to gather firewood, cook and make pottery. The women fashioned baskets of willows, cedar, tule reeds, various other bulrushes and grasses. Plant fibers were used to make cordage in the manufacture of bags, netting and rope. They made clothing, using bone or stone awls and gut for sewing.

5. Chief Quanah Parker, Comanche Shoshoni
(Photograph Courtesy of AZUSA PUBLISHING, LLC)

6. Kiowa Chief Satanta. Allies
of the Comanche
(Photograph Courtesy of
AZUSA PUBLISHING,
LLC)

Indian women were not afraid of work. The Shoshoni woman had ...ties as a wife and small children were in her care. A mother might work with ...r papoose in a cradleboard, strapped on her shoulders. The cradleboard was ...nique.

When the white men first came on the scene and saw the Shoshoni ...omen digging wild roots, they called them the "Digger Indians." They used ...igging sticks to extract the various roots from the earth.

BIG GAME

Men killed the game and brought it back for the entire extended family ...and. They skinned the animals. The women processed the animal hides. They ...repared the meat for their families. Bear meat was an excellent staple. The ...eat fed the band for a good while. The fur made nice rugs or winter coats. ...rizzly, brown and black bears haunted the Great Basin Region. The bones were ...sed for tools and the claws made fine necklaces.

Deer were best killed in the fall, when they were fatter in this season. ...eer were plentiful on the Snake River Plain and one deer would feed a small ...and for some time. The Indian being conservative prepared the whole deer.

They hunted the moose (a large herbivore). Moose also provided great ...eat. Elk was also an excellent food source for the Indians. The hides of these ...nimals were used for clothing and moccasins. The hides of these animals made ...arm clothing. The leather moccasins were more soft and supple than those ...ade from the buffalo leather. Indians used the bones for tools and the racks to ...ake weapons. Hooves were made into glue and antlers were made into tools.

The women preheated stones in a juniper or sagebrush fire until they ...ere red hot. The stones were transferred into a pitch-sealed basket containing ...ater. As the water came to a boil, meat was added to cook. Spits over a fire ...ere turned slowly turned, broiling the meat. Three slender flat rocks, called ...re-dogs, supported a pot over a fire.

Shoshoni dwelled near a creek, lake, river or hot springs to easily ...btain much needed water to bathe, cook or drink. The women drew water using ...ots or skins. A male leaving camp could carry a water-filled skin with him, like ...day's canteen, Food was normally stored in special bins underground.

SEASONAL FOOD CYCLES

In order to survive in the high desert environment the Shoshoni ...ere forced to move seasonally in order to obtain food. Men hunted and fished, ...hile the women foraged for food. The Shoshoni bands roamed with rhythm ...om one food source area to another in four seasonal cycles.

An example of how bands were named is by the food that they ate. ...heep-eater Indians depended on the mountain sheep. Mountain sheep-eater was ...hat other Shoshoni called them, for the food they ate. By combining the word, ...ater with that source of food, mountain sheep, you get mountain sheep-eater.

The main diet of the "Sheep-eater Shoshoni" was the Rocky Mountain shee[p]. The Sheep-eater hunted mountain sheep and thrived on this most nourishin[g] meat. Other Shoshoni referred to them in the seasonal cycle for the food th[ey] they ate at the time or the "Sheep-eater Shoshoni." The same applied to oth[er] foods like buffalo, salmon, etc.

In the winter, Tommo (Foreign words in this section are Shoshon[i] cycle, wind sheltered stream valleys were chosen and protected from the frig[id] wind. Fish were caught through the ice. Beaver, deer, grouse, marmot, rabb[it] sage hen and quail were also hunted for sustenance. Rabbits and other roden[ts] provided meat for the table. Jack rabbits multiplied at a rapid rate causing [a] population explosion and an abundance of rabbits everywhere. Small anima[ls] were caught in snares and sometimes deadfalls. This trap employed a heav[y] weight when the trap was triggered, fell on the prey. Ground hog was hunted b[y] catching them in their lair. By baiting a sharp hardwood hook on a line, th[e] hunter would pull up the cordage as the ground hog took the bait.

In early spring (Tahmani) during their mating season, the male sag[e] hen (hutsa) performed a mating dance by strutting in front of the hens. Th[e] roosters made off-and-on popping sounds by puffing up and releasing the ai[r] sacks on their necks. Meanwhile a Shoshoni shaman, disguised as an antelop[e] (under an antelope skin), stalked the sage grouse by crawling on all fours towar[d] them. As they moved away from him, he drove them into netting the Indians ha[d] placed over the sagebrush. The small Shoshoni community would then captur[e] the grouse for a feast.

In the spring they went up into the foothills to harvest the blue cama[s]. Camissa Quamash, the camas with the blue flower was edible. Another variet[y] with the white flower was poisonous and the Indians called it the "death plant[."] Women dug camas roots and piled them in small mounds which were sun drie[d]. The tuber was the shape of an onion. The outer layer was a black husk that wa[s] removed. The camas bulb was ground in stone mortars into meal, which wa[s] baked into camas bread.

The American bistort, bitterroot, camas and cattail are also edib[le] native plants common to the Idaho region of the Great Basin. These wild roo[ts] were dug by the Shoshoni Indians for the food value.

In summer (Tatza) fishing continued and the other foods wer[e] harvested. Women and children dug bulbs of the cat-tail, sego and water cres[s]. Wild carrots and young cattail bulbs were eaten raw. Potherbs were harveste[d] adding salad greens to their diet. Fleshy fruits and seeds were consume[d] including false dandelion, service berry, bear-berry, big sagebrush and Orego[n] grape. The pig weed (redroot), miner's lettuce, shooting star, fireweed, prickl[y] pear cactus, mountain sorrel and bracken fern were all edible and eaten. In th[e] summer they fished until the salmon season slowed in the fall. A salmo[n] festivity followed.

As autumn (Yepani) began, berries, nuts and seeds were gathered. I[n] the early fall wild rye-grass seeds were ripe. The seeds were picked an[d] separated from the husks with beaters and collected into winnowing trays an[d] thrown up in the air to separate out the chaff in the wind. Seeds were heated and dried for storage in cache pits or ground into flour before being made into Indian rye-bread. When the flowers withered on the sunflower, the seeds became exposed. The Newe (Shoshoni) women gathered them for storage. Food was stored in baskets underground and covered with green branches. They ground sunflower seeds in their mortar and pestles into flour used as gravy. Currents and buck berries were eaten off the vine, dried for the winter or were ground and made into pudding.

During Indian summer pine nuts were harvested. A celebration ritual was performed and they danced for three nights. As the dance ended, the people bathed to cleanse themselves and the shaman said a prayer to the four winds and Grandfather for a good harvest. Pine nuts were good fresh. Excess pine nuts were roasted or they might have been stored in the ground under pine boughs until they were used during the winter or ground in mortars. Flour was mixed with water making excellent gravy. As autumn ended the band of Shoshoni returned to their winter haunt to begin the next cycle. Pine nuts were an important staple to them.

FISHING

The region that became Idaho is rich with mountain lakes, rivers and streams rich in fish. River drainages were the best suited regions for aboriginal subsistence. Fishing was a big industry for the Shoshoni, as Chinook salmon swam upstream to spawn. The Salmon-eater Shoshoni dwelled along the vast Salmon River drainage in harmony with nature. Fish provided over half of their subsistence. The Northern Shoshoni caught cutthroat, rainbow and steelhead trout, sturgeon, squawfish plus Chinook salmon in the Salmon River. Numerous other drainages were selected for residence by the prehistoric Shoshoni.

The Snake River basin was a good fishing ground. Native fish that they caught were Chinook salmon, bull trout, steelhead trout, sturgeon and mountain white fish. Near Glenn's Ferry the Snake Indians used rocks to build dams, called weirs (still seen by air today) to trap Chinook salmon. With rock dams in place, the Shoshoni could catch fish with their hands or by using bone hooks, baskets, bows and arrows, nets or spears. Poison was used to stun the fish. Salmon-eaters fished the Snake River east to Shoshone Falls, with a salmon run in the spring and another in the fall. Fish provided much of their diet during this food cycle.

THE SALMON FESTIVAL

The Boise River Shoshoni lived on the Boise River drainage and had a salmon fishery at the mouth of the Boise River, yearly with plenty of Chinook salmon. They smoked large numbers of salmon on drying racks. The salmon was stored in cache pits for winter. The Shoshoni made salmon pemmican. Salmon was smoked. Dried strips of salmon were ground with berries and fat, in a mortar. This mixture was pressed into cakes, (saved in salmon skins) and cached in pits. Pemmican was also made from buffalo meat, ground in a buffalo skin mortar with a mano, to nearly a powder, mixed with chokecherries and fat and made into cakes. Woven bags were sewn out of sagebrush fibers and used to store foods underground. At the end of the salmon season, in late autumn, salmon were smoked or sun dried, placed in stacks five feet high for winter storage. In late September, the Boise Shoshonis hosted their annual Salmon Festival in the Boise Basin, where the Boise River empties into the Snake River. Bottom land along the Boise River was called "Cop-cop-pa-ala," in Shoshoni, it meant, Cottonwood Feast Valley. The Shoshoni-Bannock loved the "Peace Valley," a special place for meeting.

BUFFALO

Wild buffalo originally roamed free on the Snake River Plain as far west as the Blue Mountains in what is now Oregon. Buffalo were the largest mammal in America. They were found in America, Canada and parts of Mexico. Buffalo ranged in smaller herds, but grazed in massive herds in the summer, during mating season. Buffalo herds are made up of bulls, cows and calves, like cattle. A bull bison weighed over 2,000 pounds. Bulls fight to breed the cows. Despite their size, buffalo can run, reaching speeds of forty miles per hour.

A conservative estimation was that there were nearly 3,000,000 buffalo on the American Plains in 1860. The bison fed on grasses, sedges, and occasionally berries and lichen. They used their head and horns to clear vegetation of snow. The horse and buffalo were the salvation for the Plains Indian. Walking Shoshoni located the roving American bison herds in the wild for the hunt. Buffalo hunting for them was an art. Crawling among the wild buffalo, concealed under a buffalo robe, a brave could get a clean shot with bow and arrow. At times a decoy buffalo was used to attract a herd.

The Buffalo jump was an unusual technique of hunting. Lanes were built on a plateau with rock barriers along the sides forming a barrier. A shaman would whoop and wave a blanket. The herd grazing near the cliff would spook and stampede over the edge, to be processed into meat and hides in butchering stations. Meat from the hunt was shared. From late summer into autumn, the buffalo eaters crossed to the upper Missouri to hunt buffalo in Montana, invading Crow Indian territory. They were careful crossing Crow lands. Mountain Crow dwelled in the Bighorn Valley and the River Crow along the flowing headwaters of the Yellowstone River in Montana. Hunting parties of

Shoshoni rode in large numbers to the Upper Missouri and the Plains to hunt bison. They knew that they were vulnerable to bands of marauding Crow and Blackfoot Indians. This tribe was called Blackfoot because their moccasin soles were blackened from walking across the burned prairie.

Shoshoni would ride cautiously, silently on horseback passing single file, undetected through Blackfoot and Crow country. At any time, bands of enemy Indians might attack them. The Northern Shoshoni Indians fought the fierce Blackfoot, Crow and Sioux on their northern border.

Horse-mounted Shoshoni trekked for miles in order to reach the buffalo and follow them onto the Plains. While riding at a gallop alongside the thundering herd, the hunter could single out a choice bison. The warrior could shoot an arrow between its ribs, penetrate a lung, and drop the beast. Or, in another scenario, he might ride alongside the buffalo and bring it down with a few quick jabs of the lance. Excellent hunters with bow and lance, the warriors could kill enough buffalo to feed their extended families.

After the hunt the warriors rested before they skinned the buffalo and stretched the hides. Hides were stretched out by driving pegs into the ground around the perimeter. The women used hide-scrapers to remove flesh from the hides. The brains were removed from the skulls. Skins were tanned by rubbing the buffalo brains into the hides to process the leather. The hides were then processed in warm water. They were then hung from a tree branch about shoulder level. Hides were scraped again to give them flexibility. The hump was removed and the skin stitched up with deer sinew, using bone awls and needles.

Buffalo was the life blood of the Plains Indian. Wealth came from resources at the top of the food chain, like the buffalo, accessible with the horse. A good sized buffalo bull averaged around 2,000 pounds. Bison meat was prized. Buffalo in the Shoshoni language is "k'utsun." Women cooked the meat on spits over the fire for a feast. This was enough meat to feed the extended family for a long time. Buffalo meat was jerked and cached for the long winter. There was no waste. Hides made warm buffalo robes, winter clothing and moccasins. Buffalo skins were sewn together with sinew to make teepee coverings. Horns became spoons. Intestines made bindings to make tools and bowstrings. Hooves became glue.

The government ordered the bison killed to get the Indian onto the reservation. Bison were needlessly slaughtered by the thousands. Most of the remaining American bison now reside in Yellowstone Park.

THE HORSE

Spanish explorers brought the Appaloosa, Arabian and Barbary horses from Spain on board huge sailing ships to the American shores. They were the first modern horses on the American Continent. Ute Indians stole horses from Spanish colonists, early on. They were the first Indians to acquire horses in America. Never having seen horses, the Ute they thought horses to be big dogs.

Francisco Cortez imprisoned Ute Indians in the 1500's for stealing horses and forced them to work in the gold and silver mines.

Ute Indians stole horses from the Spaniard until the late 1600's, when the Ute entered into slave trade with the Spanish colonists. They traded slaves to the Spaniards for horses. With the advantage of the horse, the Ute Indians used the element of surprise to ride down on an Indian unsuspecting camp. Using the element of surprise, they would capture women and children from the Navajo, Shoshoni and Southern Paiute Indians, for the Spanish slave-trade. Indians tribes took captives from other tribes. It was one way of counting coup. On raids many white women and children, also were stolen for wives or slaves. Some were rescued, while others were never seen again. The Ute and Shoshoni were at odds in prehistoric times. Since historic times, the two tribes have been at peace and have entered into intermarriage.

The Comanche Indians were southern Shoshoni Plains Indians. They had migrated south, leaving the Fort Hall country around 1650, moving into what is now, Kansas. They intermarried with the Kiowa Indians, forming an alliance and a bond. Continuing south they chose the region, now known as Texas, to occupy. The Apaches raided the Spanish colonists in the late 1600's, stealing horses. The Comanche Shoshoni slipped in at night and stole horses from the Apache, an act of bravery. It was their way of counting coup. Comanche, also raided the Spanish colonists for horses.

Even though they had the horse after the Apache and Ute Indians, the Comanche became the most expert horsemen and the fiercest warriors of any tribe of Indians of the Plains. The Comanche would chase Ute horsemen, who were hunting buffalo, on the Plains and scare them off and scatter their camps. They loved their horses and sang songs to them. Comanche bred, groomed and trained their horses. They tied ribbons in their manes and braided their tails. The horsemen loved to race their horses. When a Comanche warrior died, his horses were killed and buried with him to ride in the afterlife.

#7. The beautiful Appaloosa was one of the breeds of horses brought by the Comanche Indians, to their Shoshoni cousins
(Courtesy of Jumper/Sport)

#8. Buffalo provided meat to sustain the Indians, skins for teepee walls, and buffalo robes for warmth in winter- Curtis Photo
(Courtesy of Azusa Publishing, LLC)

The Shoshoni obtained horses over 300 years ago when the Comanch' drove horses up to Fort Hall, where they traded stock to their cousin' Comanche attended the trade fair hosted by the Boise River Shoshoni, at th mouth of the Boise River and traded horses there, also. They were among th first Snake bands to acquire horses. Their horses grazed on the plush gree grasses of the Boise River bottoms, where there was good drinking wate Through the Comanche Indians, the Shoshoni tribe became a "horse nation The Cheyenne and the Mandan Indians, also had trade centers.

The Shoshoni hosted trade fair was held on a large island in the Snak River Basin, at the confluence of the Boise, Malheur, Owyhee, Payette an Weiser Rivers with the Snake River near present day Payette. Peaceable India' were welcomed from far and near in the celebrating, dancing, gambling mus and trading of arrow heads, arrows, bows, horses, knives, lodge-poles, obsidia' pelts, and other items. Coastal Indians traveled inland to the Snake River Trac Center bringing shells from the Pacific Ocean for trade. Couples met an' married there and women were traded for wives, also.

Bannock, Flathead, Nez Perce, Eastern Shoshoni Indians met at th Shoshoni Trade center to gamble and trade. The Nez Perce probably receive their first horses and acquired Appaloosa horses from the Comanche Indian Over time they bred and raised horses until their herds numbered in th thousands. It was no rare sight to see the Nez Perce trailing three or fo' hundred mounts to the Shoshoni held trade fair. The Bannock Indians, anticipation of this, brought many buffalo robes to trade them. Twenty-two Ne Perce lodges (a unit of measure), attended the Trade center. Bannock Chie Shoo-woo-koo attended.

The Bear River Shoshoni held an annual trade fair also, in the la summer, similar to the Boise River Shoshoni. Western Shoshoni attended th event, as did Chief Washakie and the Eastern Shoshoni. Buffalo hides and rob' and other articles were traded for horses. A bride cost many horses.

Discovering the horse was almost as important to the Shoshoni as th discovering of fire. Horses brought change. The Horse and Indian Era allowe the American Indian freedom of movement for war. He could travel gre distances in the hunt of the buffalo. The horse gave mobility and a good hor' race.

The style of living with the horse suited the American Indian and w' always be remembered in their hearts and minds. The Indian proved to b excellent horse handlers and raisers. The Boise Shoshoni became horse mounte early, as did the Fort Hall Shoshoni. The Mountain sheep-eater had little or r horses. Some of the Salmon-eater was horse-mounted. Weiser Shoshoni becam horse people. The Bruneau Shoshoni were sedentary fish-eaters and were n' horse mounted, until they joined the Boise River Shoshoni band.

The horse brought change to the Indian life-way. Horses were ridde in battle, work, and in the sport of racing. Indians loved their horses, but th romance between the horse and Indian was short lived. For 300 years hors' revolutionized the Amerindians' world. "The Horse and Indian Era" was a good one.

American Indians and settlers both lost horses in the early days. Mares were stolen by wild stallions or horses just strayed to run with the wild bunch (feral horses). Thousands of wild mustangs have roamed free for hundreds of years in the deserts of the American southwest.

The horse brought change to the Indian life-way. Horses were ridden, in battle, work, and in the sport of racing. Indians loved their horses, but the romance between the horse and Indian was short lived. For 300 years horses revolutionized the Amerindians' world. "The Horse and Indian Era" was a good one.

American Indians and settlers both lost horses in the early days. Mares were stolen by wild stallions or horses just strayed to run with the wild bunch (feral horses). Thousands of wild mustangs have roamed free for hundreds of years in the deserts of the American southwest. A stampeding herd of mustangs is a sight to see.

WARFARE

As the young brave became a man, instead of warfare, he learned to count coup. A coup stick was usually a tree sapling about 3-4 feet long that had been soaked in water and bent into a curved crook. The stick was decorated with feathers and paint. The brave would run or ride at a gallop toward his opponent, giving war-whoops, strike him with his quirt or coup stick, then depart. This showed bravery, by getting in his enemies' face.

All this changed in actual combat that could mean loss of life. Scalping was learned from the French. Many scalps were taken. The French scalp was about the size of a silver dollar and included the hair and scalp. Other means of scalping took the full scalp with hair. Usually the scalps were taken from enemies killed in battle. The number of scalps was another method of counting coup to show bravery. The custom spread throughout the tribes, however, some tribes, like the Nez Perce refused to scalp in battle.

The Blackfoot Indians dwelled west of the Great Lakes before migrating onto the Montana Plains. They roamed into the region that became Idaho. Blackfoot Indians would raid anytime they thought they could acquire Shoshoni ponies. They warred on neighboring tribes. They were a major threat to the Bannock and Shoshoni. Northern Shoshoni kept a constant vigil for thieving Blackfoot raiders. These were fierce Indians that would attack a band just for their horses. Blackfoot warriors were afraid of none, a powerful foe hated by the neighboring tribes.

EXPLORERS MEET THE SHOSHONI

Captain Gray, American commander of the "Columbia," with his ship was a trader within Puget Sound on the Washington coast. He traded for furs with the coastal Indians. In 1792 Gray discovered the mouth of the Columbia River where he managed to enter the Columbia and sail up river for several miles.

The Lewis and Clark party spent the winter of 1804 in Fort Mandan and while there, Toussaint Charbonneau, a French-Indian fur trapper, greeted them. They hired him as interpreter and met his wife, Sacajawea. The word, Sacajawea means "Bird Woman," in the Shoshoni language. As a teenager Sacajawea, a Lemhi Shoshoni, was stolen by the Hidatsa Indians. Charbonneau later won Sacajawea in a gambling game with the Indians and took her as his third wife, in Indian tradition. At the fort that winter, Sacajawea gave birth to their son, Baptiste. Lewis and Clark nicknamed him, Pompey.

In the spring of 1805, they left Fort Mandan and canoed up the Missouri River, through "grizzly country," to its headwaters. The Corp descended the western slopes of the Rocky Mountains. Low on supplies, they counted on reaching Sacajawea's people for help. "Fort Colt Killed Camp" was the site where Lewis and Clark were forced to kill a young colt to keep them from starvation.

Sacajawea began to recognize landmarks of the high mountain valley haunt of her people. Gradually Northern Shoshoni Indians became visible as their camp was reached. Cameahwait was chief of the Lemhi Shoshoni. He was pleasantly surprised when a party of famous white men ("Taibo," in Shoshoni) visited his region. The chief was more than surprised when a member of the exploration party turned out to be Sacajawea, his sister, who had been stolen by the Hidatsa Indians. Recognizing her brother, she rushed toward Chief Cameahwait and began sucking her fingers, the Shoshoni sign of kinship. The reunion was a gala affair!

Sacajawea spoke no English, only the Shoshoni and Hidatsa dialects. She and her husband worked as a team. Sacajawea translated Shoshoni into Hidatsa while Charbonneau knew Hidatsa and translated the message into French. There was a French speaker in the Lewis and Clark party who also spoke English. That way the interpreters, Charbonneau and Sacajawea could successfully translate between Lewis and Clark and the Shoshoni Indians. Lewis and Clark sat cross-legged and traded with the Shoshoni. Clark was able to get provisions, pack horses and also, Old Toby, a Shoshoni guide. The Lewis and Clark Party said goodbye to the Shoshoni for the time being. Canoes were cached, for the return trip, by sinking them with big rocks.

9. An American Indian Wickiup
(Courtesy of the Library of
Congress)

#10. Ancient Indian petroglyphs on rock walls in Idaho.
(Author photo)

In August of 1804, Pierre Dorion (also spelled Dorian) Jr. was introduced to Lewis and Clark along the Missouri by his father. Pierre Dorion Jr. had been trapping on the James River and trading with the Yankton Sioux Indians at the time. Marie was an Iowa Sioux Indian born in a teepee on the banks of the Missouri River. She married Pierre Dorion, Jr., who was a French-Sioux Indian cross who spoke Sioux. A Sioux interpreter was needed and in 1811 Pierre signed on with the Wilson Price Hunt's party of fur traders in St. Louis, as interpreter asking that his family could join them.

The Hunt Party departed St. Louis and paddled up the Missouri River in dugout canoes, reached an Arikara Indian village, where they cached their canoes. Hunt bartered with the Arikara and the Crow Indians for horses. They crossed the Bighorn Mountains to the Wind River in Wyoming Territory in 18 days. Hunt again traded for new mounts with the Cheyenne Indians, trade partners of the Arikara Indians. They crossed Union Pass to the Green River valley. They traded with Shoshoni Indians for jerky. They hunted buffalo and jerked around two tons of meat. Crossing the Hobart River Valley Basin, the party reached the Snake River. Deciding not to build dugouts, they continued on horseback.

Crossing the Continental Divide they rode on southwest to Jackson's Hole and hiked out of the Teton Range. Four traders remained to trap beaver, near Three Forks, in the spring of 1812. Crow Indian raiders attacked and killed one trapper. Two Shoshoni Indians guided the party across the Snake River, up Fall Creek, and over Teton Pass, again crossing the Continental Divide. They rode on horseback to Pierre's Hole. They gained dugouts and floated down the north fork of the Snake River (Henry's Fork). The party lost canoes and one man drowned at Caldron Lynn. Hiking three days without water along the Snake River Canyon into now Idaho, Marie suffered from exhaustion and thirst. The party reached what is now Hagerman Valley, where they found precious drinking water. Hunt's party had made it over the Rockies!

Near what is now Eagle, Idaho they met Shoshoni Indians who shared fresh puppy meat with them. Pierre traded with the Indians for a much needed horse and was later forced to dismount and surrender the horse to Marie and the boys. The party split into three groups led by Hunt, McKenzie and Crooks. They reached Astoria, May 11, 1812. The group's fur shipments to England were jeopardized by the War of 1812.

A year later, in 1813 Pierre and Marie were back at the mouth of the Boise River working for Reed (also spelled, Reid) of the Astoria group. Reed's winter trading post was erected, that year on the east side of the Snake River near the confluence of the Boise River. La Chapelle, Le Clerc, Dorion and Rezner lived in a cabin (lean-to or hut) Reed had built to hunt the beaver. He had abandoned the original Fort Boise (cabin) since unruly Indians often came demanding guns. In 1814, a band of warring Bannock burned down the abandoned cabin and continued down the Boise River whooping and chanting war-songs.

Marie was skinning beaver at Reed's cabin, 15 miles east of the burned cabin, on the north side of the Boise River near what is now Notus, Idaho. At the time, a friendly Indian woman informed her that the warring Dog-ribs (Bannock) Indians were coming up river. Marie rode with her boys up stream to find Pierre. She camped overnight and stayed there the next day because of bad weather. Seeing a smoke signal sent up by the Bannock, she remained there. Marie was near what is now Table Rock, which was called "Ala-Kush-pa." It was an excellent observation point for the Indians to survey enemies and to send smoke signals to their tribe.

Marie found Le Clerc barely alive. After he told her of the massacred Reed party, she hoisted him up onto her horse, but he fell off several times. As she approached the main cabin, Marie saw Indians gallop off near the river ford. Le Clerk died and she buried him outdoors under snow and brush. When she reached the cabin, Marie found her husband's body, scalped and mutilated.

The children were now cold and hungry. She built a fire. Marie returned to the cabin, armed only with a knife and tomahawk. She saw wolves eating their kill, and scared them off. Marie found a fresh supply of fish in the cabin and hurried back to the boys. Stoking the fire, Marie added more wood. She cooked the fish and they ate for the first time in three days. She rested a few days with her sons. Marie loaded supplies onto her horse. With the death of her husband, Marie took her boys on horseback and crossed the Snake River and began her long trek to the Pacific Ocean and Fort Astoria. She headed over the snow covered Blue Mountains. When the going got rough, Marie located an overhang and built a fire. She kept her boys warm in their rabbit fur robes, near the fire. Surviving the winter on berries, nuts and small rodents, like rabbit. When those resources were depleted, Marie killed her horse for food to stay alive. She trudged westward for days, with her papoose in a cradleboard, strapped to her back and held on to Baptiste's hand. Marie was snow-blind and exhausted when they reached the Umatilla Indians and were finally rescued.

Marie and Sacajawea once met, in 1811, as the Manual Lisa Party overtook the Hunt party. The famous heroines had much in common. Marie was Iowa Sioux, while Sacajawea was Lemhi Shoshoni. Charbonneau and Pierre Jr. were French Canadian fur traders of French-Indian cross. Both women had sons named Baptiste. Both women crossed America from St. Louis to the Pacific with famous men. The two brought infants along on their journey. Their husbands were interpreters for Lewis and Clark and the Hunt Party. Pierre's father was interpreter for Lewis and Clark. Marie Dorion remarried twice and lived out her life in Oregon with her new family. She died, September 5, 1850.

THE FUR TRADE

Fur Trade Companies from America, England, France, Russia and Spain engaged in the trade. Individual mountain men like Jim Bridger and Kit Carson were fur traders. Mountain men John Colter and George Droulliard were fur trapping legends by the time that they joined the Manuel Lisa party with the St.

Louis Missouri Fur Trade Company, around 1809-10. At the Three Forks of the Missouri in the spring of 1810, they assisted in building "Henry's Fort" on Henry's Fork, on the north fork of the Snake River.

France, Great Britain and Spain fought to control the Pacific Northwest. On October 20, 1818, Britain and the United States signed a treaty to jointly occupy the Northwest Territory over a ten year period. Early in 181 Spain ceded her right to Idaho Territory.

McKenzie held a trade rally with his trappers, the Bannock and Shoshoni Indians. Meeting with Chief Peiem and other Shoshoni Chiefs McKenzie paved the way for trapping in the region. He reached the Indians remote regions on snowshoes, in deep snow. Donald McKenzie worked for the Astoria, North West and Hudson's Bay Companies. He crossed over the Blue Mountains with a large trapping brigade. McKenzie left six Iroquois Indians the second Fort Boise with food, gear and traps. McKenzie took a brigade boats, up the Snake River. He dropped off trappers at outposts, reaching the Bear River.

When McKenzie returned to "Fort Boise" he found that the Iroquois had deserted to local Indian villages. The trappers regrouped with the Iroquois Fort Boise. McKenzie held a rendezvous there, in 1819. A year later he held peace talks on the Little Lost River with the Shoshoni. Hudson's Bay Company rivaled American fur companies in the Snake River region. Employees, Peter Scene Ogden, Alexander Ross and John Work trapped the Snake River Plain early.

French trappers named the river, "Riviera Bois" or Boise River. "Bois meaning wooded area in French, was the source of the name, Boise City. The Boise River was utilized by the Shoshoni Indians and French trappers for years French traders named local rivers such as the Malheur, Weiser and the Payette Rivers. The Payette River was named for Captain Francois Payette.

Russia ceded all her rights to the Pacific Northwest, in 1824. John McLoughlin founded Fort Vancouver, headquarters for the Hudson's Bay Company in northwestern America and Oregon City. He was commissioned General Manager to build "Fort Vancouver," in 1825 on the north bank of the Columbia River, the center of trade in the western hemisphere.

#11. The statue of Sacajawea rests at the entrance to the Boise Historical Museum in Boise, Idaho. As a teenager, Sacajawea, a Lemhi Shoshoni, was taken captive by the Hidatsa Indians. Charbonneau won Sacajawea in a gambling game with the Indians and took her as his third wife, in Indian tradition (Author Photo)

Chief Factor McLoughlin was in charge of 34 outposts, 24ports, six ships, and 600 employees, including many Hawaiians, Chelas, Cree, and Iroquois Indians. During the 1820's, brigades of Hudson's Bay trappers pushed south from Vancouver, along the Siskiyou trail, into the San Francisco Bay Region. In 1828, Britain renewed the ten year treaty with America. By 1830, the Hudson's Bay Company had control of the fur trade.

Hudson's Bay Company chose the uncharted region that would become Idaho as the site for their fur trade fort. John McLoughlin selected Thomas McKay to go and build the fort. McKay chose a fort location on Idaho Territory's western border, at the site where Reed and McKenzie had their forts. The Shoshoni held their salmon fishery at the mouth of the Boise River for years. The Shoshoni warned McKay not to build the fort there; that the river would "change its mind." This prophecy would come to haunt him. Fort Boise, Fort Hall and Fort Laramie fur forts were also erected, in 1834.

Furs were traded by the Indians. In return Hudson's Bay traders bartered beads, brass rings, burning glasses, calico shirts, coats and caps, gunpowder, red & blue kersey cloth, kettles, knives, lace, powder horns, rings of brass wire, red Gloucester, scimitars, thread, tinsel, twine and yarn stockings. The beautifully colored Hudson's Bay blanket was a favorite traded for by the Indians. Other goods traded included numerous varieties of glass, shell, and stone beads. The Hudson's Bay Company was a highly successful operation, the oldest corporation in North America.

Fort Boise, Fort Hall and Fort Laramie fur forts were erected, in 1834. Fort Hall was a stockade fort built by Nathaniel Wyeth, 300 miles east of Fort Boise. Wyeth's luck was bad and he wound up selling the fur trade post to the Hudson's Bay Company. By 1856 the fort was abandoned. When Fort Hall closed, it served as an Indian school for Shoshoni-Paiute Indian children.

In 1834 Thomas McKay built "Fort Snake." Thomas constructed the edifice out of wood. The Hudson's Bay Company bankrolled McKay and hired him as a factor, in the position of clerk. John Finley was the first Postmaster at Fort Snake. The fort was built, in 1834 by the Hudson's Bay Company. It served as both general store and trading post. A ferry and a stage stop would be added to the fort, later. Furs were traded by Western Shoshoni and Northern Paiute Indians. In 1834, the fort showed a profit of 300 pounds.

Hudson's Bay Trappers hunted beaver in brigades, bringing their furs to Old Fort Snake, as did independent trappers and Indians. Hudson's Bay Company appointed a chief trader to oversee trapping on the Snake River Plain for one year. John McKay preferred leading brigades to other duties.

The fort was described as a stockade, with cool water, a hot spring, a garden, a pasture for the horses, a green grassy valley, cottonwood trees and Indian teepees, as part of the landscape. Fish were plentiful, there. It became an important stop along the Oregon Trail for emigrants who needed supplies and for wagon trains fording the Snake there. It was a central location for the Indian and white people alike.

In 1842, John Freemont observed many lodges along the Boise River. He referred to them as "Shoshonee or Snake Indians." In 1860, Boise River Shoshoni lodges on the Camas Prairie, numbered 75 lodges and a large number of horses. Their chief was Amaroko (Buffalo MeatUnder the Shoulder).

Jim Bridger was an Indian fighter. He fought the Arikara and the Blackfeet, who were fierce foes. He spoke several Indian dialects, besides knowing the Indian sign language.

A legendary story was told about Jim Bridger. When Blackfoot Indians caught Jim trapping in their territory, he took flight, retreating, his horse in a full gallop. A small band of angry Blackfeet Indians was in hot pursuit of him. Jim headed for his fort and rode for his life, his horse lathered. Jim managed to stay alive and keep his scalp, but caught an arrow in the back. He survived for three years with the arrow-head in his backbone. Finally, Dr. Marcus Whitman removed it without anesthetic.

Jim Bridger was a frontiersman, who lived among the Indians. As was their custom, he took three Native American wives. He first married a Flathead woman. She bore him three children. Then Jim married a Ute Indian woman and took a third wife, in Indian fashion. She was the daughter of Goshute Shoshoni Chief Washakie, chief of the Green River and Wind River Shoshoni bands in Wyoming Territory. She gave birth to two children. One daughter was a student at the Whitman Mission School in Oregon.

After trapping for two decades, Bridger built "Fort Bridger," with a partner, Louis Vasquez, located on Black's Fork of the Green River, in early Wyoming (1843). Fort Bridger became a major way station along the Oregon Trail. They traded furs with the Indians, mountain men and sold goods to the immigrants.

During his lifetime, Jim Bridger served as a guide for the U.S. Army, the Union Pacific Railroad and the Overland Stage Company. He quarreled with Mormons in Salt Lake City and eventually sold them his fort.

CHIEF WASHAKIE

The U.S. Army referred to the Wyoming Territory Goshute Shoshoni under Chief Washakie as the Eastern Shoshoni. The father of Chief Washakie was a Salish Flathead. His mother was a Lemhi Shoshoni.

Washakie was chief of the Green and Wind River Shoshoni of western Wyoming. The two bands numbered around 2,000 Goshutes (cat-tail eaters). A peaceable Shoshoni, Washakie cooperated with the white man. He is also credited for bravery, taking six enemy Indian scalps and counting coup.

The daughter of Chief Washakie married the famous mountain man, Jim Bridger. Eastern Shoshoni extended from Utah and Wyoming Territories into Colorado Territory. Jim married three American Indian wives in the Indian tradition. He was a true frontiersman and scout.

A favorite legend of the Shoshoni Indians is the story of the white son of Chief Washakie. This is a true story that occurred in Wyoming Territory, in 1859.

Two children, a brother and sister ran away from Fort Bridger with intentions of playing with Indian children. Crossing a meadow, the boy named Hiram was taken captive by an Indian on horseback, the girl escaped.

The Shoshoni warrior took the boy to the village and teepee of Washakie, presenting the boy to him. Washakie was delighted with him and decided to adopt the boy. The chief gave him four ponies and dressed him in Indian regalia. The women braided and adorned his hair. The chief loved the boy and raised him for five years. Washakie warned the boy to stay away from whites, but one evening Hiram mounted his pony and rode down into Salt Lake.

The blonde haired Indian was discovered sleeping in a barn, wrapped in a bearskin robe. He was wearing a breech-clout, leggings beaded deerskin shirt and long blonde braids. Hiram was soon reunited with his step-father and family.

Hiram learned that his sister, for fear that Indians would take her, had been placed on a wagon train for the Whitman Mission and never heard from again. The family traveled along the Platte River, where large herds of buffalo could be seen in Nebraska Territory traveling to St. Louis. Later, he and his friend Felix Bridger, son of Jim Bridger served as water carriers on a wagon-train to Santa Fe.

As a young man, Hiram embarked on his own, finding work at a settlement in La Veta, Colorado for Colonel Francisco. When the settlement was surrounded by 1,000 Ute warriors, led by Chief Kanache, Hiram became a hero by riding out at night and bringing back the Cavalry from Fort Lyon, on the Arkansas River.

THE WAGON TRAINS

The missionaries, Marcus and Narcissa Prentiss Whitman with Henry nd Eliza Spalding, had traveled overland from New York, reaching Fort Boise, 1836. Whitman's was the first wagon to cross the plains. Whitman's wagon d broken down on the trail. The useless remnant was abandoned at the old rt. The Hudson's Bay people took the Whitman's and Spalding's from the fort est into Oregon. Marcus Whitman headed up a massive wagon train into regon, in 1843. Thousands of emigrants followed.

After 1843, Euro-American emigrants embarked in vast numbers on the ng 2,000 mile journey west from St. Louis to California and Oregon Territory. omen and children rode in the wagons, while others rode horses or mules. ome simply walked along the wagons. Emigrant wagon trains dotted the orizon for miles. A number of wagons joined together in a wagon train. There as safety in numbers. Guides were employed to lead the wagons. A vote etermined train captain and other officers. At night, wagons were formed in a rcle or corral and guards were posted for security.

Three Island crossing was a major junction of the Oregon Trail and the nake River, yet one of the most dangerous river crossings on the Oregon Trail. ater, grass and firewood were available. Glenn's Ferry, a small town near ere, was named after Gus Glenn, who owned and operated the river ferry. lenn ferried hundreds of wagons across the treacherous Snake River. Others rded the river across the gravel sandbars and followed the northern route. ome of the wagons continued along the south side of the Snake River, the uthern route of the Oregon Trail. It was a much more rugged trip. Thousands f pioneers passed this way. Sometimes, emigrants waited until late July or ugust to cross the Snake River after the water level had gone down. Not all of e wagons crossed the river successfully, as was recorded in emigrant diaries. he two trails would not intersect again until reaching old Fort Boise.

There were two types of covered wagons: the Conestoga wagon and the airie Schooner. The Conestoga wagon was manufactured first. The heavier onestoga had broader wheels than the Prairie Schooner and was more mbersome. The Prairie Schooner weighed just one ton. It outlived the onestoga. Prairie Schooners were compared to sailing ships, moving on the cean.

The great Oregon Trail and the Mormon Trail became main routes for ousands of travelers. Because of rumors that white men were planning their emise, Indians began raiding wagon trains and stage lines. As American ttlers traveled west by wagon train, they were attacked by Indians. In 1851, irmishes were fought between the Indians and the emigrants. Thirty two white ople were killed that year. As emigrants continued to the West, Indian Wars upted.

Emigrants feared the Indians. Military forts were direly needed for otection. The army hoped to establish a military garrison in the Boise Valley, an extension of Fort Vancouver.

In 1853 the Walker War broke out between Ute Chief Walkara an Brigham Young's Mormons in Utah territory. The same year a peace treaty wa signed with the combatants. In 1853 a two year siege began with the Rogu River Indian War.

In 1854 a Sioux Indian killed a Mormon's cow at Fort Larami Lieutenant Grattan decided to teach the Sioux a lesson. He led his troops an rode into Sioux Indian country. All of the U.S. Army soldiers were killed b Sioux Indians. The Grattan Massacre occurred along the Platte River country.

The first treaty between the Plains Indians and the America government was signed at Fort Laramie. It assigned boundaries to the tribes, y Indians constantly raided wagon trains and stage lines.

THE WARD MASSACRE

In August 1854, a wagon train moved slowly westward along the Bois River on the Oregon Trail. Their next stop was Fort Boise on the Snake Rive The Ward wagon train of 23 people left the other wagons, electing to have picnic along the Boise River and unhitched their wagons just south o Middleton, Idaho.

Older brother, Robert Ward ran into camp. He shouted, "Indians hav stolen a horse," and all hell erupted. Hitching up their horses, the Ward par pulled their rigs onto the road, trying to escape. They were immediate surrounded by 200 Snake Indians. The Indians approached and pretended to b trading horses. A shot rang out. Wagon-master, Alexander Ward, fell from h wagon, mortally wounded. Arrows and bullets flew. By sunset, all of the adu males in the party were murdered. The warriors overpowered the remainir women and children in the party that were left alive. Mrs. Ward, her teen-ag daughter and two little girls were tortured and killed. Three children ju vanished.

Sometimes, renegades took white women and children captive fo brides or slaves; some were never seen again. The Indians burned the wago and fled. During the attacks the teen-age Ward boys, both struck by arrow crawled into the brush and escaped. William, showing much bravery, walke miles to Fort Boise, with an arrow in his lung. Newton was later found alive! A this time, it was discovered that the British traders at Fort Boise had been sellir guns and ammunition to the Indians. Traders often sold whiskey to the Indian which did not help the situation. Snake Indians were blamed for the massacre.

At Fort Dalles, in Oregon Territory, Major Rains ordered Haller and 2 soldiers to pursue the renegades. Some thirty nine volunteers, under Natha Olney, with a number of Nez Perce and Umatilla Indians, rode behind the U.S Cavalry. Arriving at the massacre site Haller buried 18 bodies. He found the trail into the mountains. He discontinued the search for the time, since winte was coming. They caught and lynched eighteen of the Indians responsible fo the attacks, the exact number killed in the Ward massacre. The Ward Massacr Memorial on the old Oregon Trail is a monument of the Ward massacre.

In 1855, it was reported that there were some 1500 Shoshoni at Green River while 700 Shoshoni, 200 Bannock and 300 Sheep-eater Shoshoni lived at Fort Hall. By 1856, Fort Hall closed and served as an Indian School for the Shoshoni-Paiute Indian children.

Shortly after the Ward Massacre, three white men were killed by Indians. It was becoming too dangerous to remain at Fort Boise and Fort Hall. This occurrence was followed by the Modoc Indian uprising, in Oregon Territory in 1855. In Washington Territory they fought the Yakima Indian tribe, in 1856.

In 1855, Mormon missionaries arrived, and erected Fort Lemhi, among the Salmon-eater and Sheep-eater Shoshoni. Lemhi valley was the home of Sacajawea and her Lemhi band. They were the same Lemhi Shoshoni that entertained Lewis and Clark. Mormon missionaries renamed these two bands, the Lemhi Shoshoni. Chief Snag (Tio-van-du-ah) was baptized into the Mormon Church on November 11, 1855. Many Mormons were urged to take Indian women as brides. Chief Tendoy was a peace loving Lemhi chief. He voluntarily went onto the reservation.

In 1857, Kit Carson and Jim Bridger and several trappers were attacked by 50 Bannock Indians, while traveling from Montana to Fort Hall. Kit received a shoulder wound.

Sparked by the Utah War of 1857, Fort Lemhi was attacked by a band of Shoshoni, in 1858. Shortly thereafter, the Mormon missionaries left that region.

RAIDS IN EASTERN IDAHO TERRITORY

The Palouse Indians in northern Idaho Territory executed raids, in 1858. The Yakima Indian Wars were fought with the Euro-Americans, from 1855-1858. The Army defeated the Yakima Indians in 1858 and confined them to a reservation, in 1859.

Some bands of Indians sometimes just followed behind wagon trains. The settlers could not determine if the Indians were peaceful or warlike. It was not clear whether the Indians were sizing them up or just curious. From 1860-1863, the Snakes made a series of raids on wagon trains in eastern Idaho Territory.

On October 16, 1860, Snake renegades massacred the Utter Party Wagon train, west of Castle Butte in early Owyhee County, Idaho. On August 9, 1862, emigrants traveled westward. The Smart wagon train was followed by the Adams, Wilson and Kennedy trains. One half mile from Massacre Rocks, a Snake war-party ambushed the Smart wagons and massacred the Adam's train. They attacked and killed settlers, stole their livestock and burned their wagons, killing ten emigrants, total. A Smallpox epidemic killed one third of the Indian population in British Columbia in 1862.

41

United States President Abraham Lincoln ordered the U.S. Army to the western front to protect the emigrant wagon trains, miners and settlers from Indian attacks.

Idaho became a territory in 1863 and an Indian agent was assigned to the Bannock and Shoshoni Indians. The agent had been previously assigned in the Oregon and Washington territories.

CHIEF POCATELLO

Chief Pocatello of the Bear River Shoshoni rebelled against white men that intruded on their lands. He disliked those who did not respect his people. The chief had remained hostile to the white man entering Shoshoni Territory from the beginning. His camp lay between the junction of the California Trail and the Salt Lake Road. Passing emigrants fired on his people and killed them at random. If an enemy tribe, like the Blackfoot Indians, entered their borders, the Shoshoni would have attacked them. In the same way, Pocatello avenged the deaths of his people.

Chief Pocatello attacked many of the wagon trains moving west. Emigrants killed game where his Shoshoni usually hunted. White settlers used Shoshoni water holes for their livestock, exhausting the supply. Their cattle grazed plants and grasses down to nothing. Seeds that the Shoshoni gathered for food were destroyed. Game could not forage on what the cattle left behind.

The white man killed the game that remained and left the Indians nothing. Pocatello suffered when thousands of emigrants crossed this people's land. He could not bear to see the people in his band face starvation. In the winter, Pocatello camped near Indian agents in order to get their food ration. The white people continued to come by the thousands. Indian agents and Army officers had heard of Chief Pocatello and his Shoshoni band, even U.S. President Abraham Lincoln.

Pocatello was chief of over 300 Shoshoni Indians camped at Bear River. He was a brave leader of his people, feared by the military, Indian agents and settlers. Pocatello stood up to Army officers. In August of 1859 Conner arrested Pocatello. He would not admit making raids on Ben Holiday's stage stops to General Conner.

U. S. Army Colonel P.E. Conner and his company of soldiers rode to Camp Bear River and issued an order that demanded the Shoshoni to turn over the braves that had raided and killed emigrants.

Chief Pocatello left Bear River the day prior to Conner's attack. He took Chief Sagwitch and as many Shoshoni with him as would leave and escape to safety. Chief Bear Hunter and other sub-chiefs refused to join Pocatello and leave Bear River. They had taken Conner's demands lightly.

#12. "Old Fort Boise" Artist's rendition
by prominent Boise Artist, Len Sodenkamp

Nearly 300 Shoshoni died the next day, including men, women and children. The Army finally arrested Pocatello that year and put him in irons, but soon, released him. After that, the chief avoided the Army officers as much as he could. He always refused to become complacent and fit the passive mode. Pocatello and his band did not want to farm. Pocatello thought that it was women's work. He was independent and did not want to give up Indian lands. The chief wanted to live as he always had.

The U.S. Army was called in. Major Lugenbeel established Camp River Boise, in 1863. It was established at the time of the Civil War. Camp River Boise was an outpost used to fight the Indians. Both Camp River Boise and Boise City were raised at the same time. Camp River Boise was later known as Fort Boise. The fort was an extension of Fort Vancouver. With the Civil War winding down, Indian fighters arrived at the fort. The U.S. Army often engaged the Indians in combat. As soon an uprising would break out and was put down, while another occurred. Indian Wars continued but the Amerindians were defeated.

Comanche Indians had fought the white man during the Texas-Indian Wars, since 1840. The Comanche and Southern Plains Indians had resisted the white Eyes' advance for years, fighting the Texas Rangers. The Texas-Indian Wars coincided with the Black Hawk War in Utah. The Treaty of Medicine Lodge was signed between the U.S. Army and the Comanche, the Cheyenne and the Plains Apache Indians, in October of 1867.

The Army began moving the Idaho Indians onto reservations by 1870. They confiscated the Indians' guns and shot their horses to limit movement. The last of the combatants were relocated onto government reserves. Peace had not come easy. Indian agents taught them to farm and provided seed to plant.

Mountain Sheep-eater, Shoshoni Chief Eagle-Eye and his band neglected to go onto the reservation at the time. General Howard pursued Eagle-Eye during the Snake War in 1866, but the Army quit looking for him after a false report of his death. He chose to remain on the land around Dry Buck and Timber Butte, an old obsidian source of the Shoshoni, near present day Emmet, Idaho.

#13. An Eastern Shoshoni Indian Village of
Chief Washakie, of the Green and Wind River tribes
(Chief stands in center) (Courtesy of the Smithsonian Institute)

He and his people engaged in the mining and timber business and were friendly to the white man. He remained there until 1904, before going to the Fort Hall Reservation.

In 1871 the U.S. Congress ended the process of treaties with the Indians. From 1871-1879, the American government sponsored the wholesale slaughter of bison herds to force the Plains Indians onto reservations. 1872-187 the Modoc War was fought over Indian lands. After many battles, the Modoc Indians retreated onto a reservation. Modoc Chief, Captain Jack was capture and executed for the murder of General Canby.

From 1865-1872, the Black Hawk War was waged between the Ute Paiute and Navajo Indians. The war was led by Chief Black Hawk. In 1872 the Utah War with the Mormons drew to a close. In 1873, a Comanche medicine man named, Isatai made a prophecy. He said that the buffalo would return if the Comanche Indians killed the white intruders. The Red River War of 1874 was fought between the U.S. Cavalry and the Arapaho, Comanche, Kiowa and Southern Cheyenne was fought on the Southern Plains. Chief Quanah Parker surrendered in 1875, after leading the Comanche. Parker and 400 warriors were the last to relent. On June 2, 1875, they entered Fort Sill, driving 1500 head of horses onto the reservation. The Southern Plains Shoshoni Indians surrendered and agreed to dwell on reservations.

SHOSHONE-BANNOCK RESERVATIONS

The Shoshone-Bannock Fort Hall Indian Reservation is located in southeastern Idaho, eight miles north of Pocatello. The reservation was established by the Fort Bridger Treaty of 1868. The Shoshoni Indians at Fort Hall were given 1.8 million acres, initially by the Great White Father, President of the United States. This has been reduced to 544,000 acres. Every adult Indian was given 160 acres. 80 acres was given to each child. A seven member council was established in 1936, with a law and order code called the Fort Hall Business Council. There are presently, 3500 Indians residing at Fort Hall, with 5,000 actual members. The tribe has a tribal credit bureau, employment agency and recreation organization.

Duck Valley Indian Reservation was first established in 1877 and enlarged in 1886. This Shoshone-Paiute Reservation lies on the Idaho-Nevada border, half in each state, in Owyhee County, Idaho and Elko County, Nevada. The Shoshone-Paiute Tribes maintain 289,820 acres of land. 1,265 Native Americans were living on the Duck Valley Indian Reservation in year, 2,000 There is little evidence of agriculture among the Shoshoni Indians until historic times. Some farming occurred with the Northern Paiute Tribe. The Shoshoni Indians did learn to farm after the white man moved them onto to the reservations.

In prehistoric times some tribes planted beans, corn and squash. Today, agriculture is the main income resource. The Indians farm 87,000 acres. Cattle and horses graze there. Sheep Creek and Mountain View Reservoirs provide fishing on the reservation. A third reservoir, the Billie Shaw, is being prepared. Shore birds and waterfowl flock to the wetland areas in great numbers. The public can camp, bird watch, fish or just relax and enjoy this recreation area.

The Wind River Reservation was established for the Eastern Shoshoni Indians. Chief Winnemucca's tribe, the Eastern Shoshoni, is located on the Wind River Reservation. The reserve occupies over two million acres in central Wyoming. Wind River is home to both the Northern Arapaho and the Eastern Shoshoni Indians. Each tribe has its own government. The Eastern Shoshoni number 2,650 Indians. There are 1,702 people in tribal headquarters. Sixty percent of the Indians there have high school diplomas and 6% have at least Bachelor Degrees.

Gold was discovered in Idaho in 1862, in the Boise Basin and along the Salmon River. This was in the Lemhi Shoshoni country. The boon brought thousands of prospectors onto Shoshoni lands. They swarmed over Shoshoni country, including the winter haunts of the Mountain Sheep-eater Shoshoni. The Indians became agitated and were a constant menace to the miners. The Sheep-eaters were accused of stealing cattle from settlers at Prairie Basin, in 1879. Two prospectors were killed near Warren's Ranch, outside of Cascade. Five Chinese were killed by Loon Creek, eighty miles north east of Boise. The town of Oro Grande was set on fire and the town gutted.

It was presumed that it was the Indians' doing. General Howard feared that fugitive Bannock and Nez Perce had joined together with the Sheep-eater Shoshoni for a fight. The Sheep-eater War began on May 31, 1879. Colonel Bernard and his Company G, 1st Cavalry left Boise Barracks, riding hard north to intercept the warring Sheep-eaters. There were only two skirmishes in that war. At the end only 51 Sheep-eater War men, women and children were taken prisoners. Those who chose war found themselves to be engaged with the Cavalry. Their fight was short lived. In 1880, the U.S. government banned the "Sun Dance" in order to force the Indians to accept the American culture.

#14. Fort Hall Drawing, an artist's rendition by Len Sodenkamp.

#15. In 1842, Covered wagon trains left St. Louis on a large scale. Conestoga covered wagons were the popular mode of travel on the Oregon Trail west to Oregon Territory. (Courtesy of the Idaho State Historical Society)

Chapter Two
BANNOCK INDIANS

The Bannock (Bannack) Indians evolved from the Northern Paiute Tribe. Northern Paiute Indians drifted down into the southwest corner of the region now known as Idaho. The Shoshoni Indians called them the "Bannock." They were an offshoot of the Paiute, a small tribe, never numbering much over one thousand people. The Shoshoni Indians called them Panati or Ba-naite, meaning, "people from below." The Bannock called themselves, Pah'ahnuck translated, "from across the water." Passed from generation to generation was the story that their ancestors traversed a long way across the water to arrive in America. One possible source of the word Bannock comes from two Shoshoni words, Bamb (hair) and (nack) backwards motion or Bampnack, translated (Bannock). Bannock Indians refer to themselves as "the people."

The Bannock and Shoshoni Indian tribes linguistically were both of the Uto-Aztecan language stock. Their dialects differed. The Bannock and Shoshoni tribes were both Numic speakers, but the Bannock people's dialect was closer to the Northern Paiute language. The Bannock, Shoshoni and Northern Paiute tribes were all grouped into the same category called "Snake or Digger Indians." Bannock Indians were taller in stature than Shoshoni and more light skinned, like the Nez Perce. At the time of the white man's coming, they confused the Bannock with the Northern Paiute, farther west.

The Bannock's lineage passed through the father's line, like the Shoshoni. Polygamy was practiced in marriage, common among Bannock Indians in their prehistory. A man marrying an Indian bride would also take her younger sisters for wives, and all could dwell in the same lodge. Non-related wives were forced to dwell in other lodges and an Indian bride could marry a man, and then marry his younger brother, etc.

In later times, the Bannock became monogamous. If the wife died, the husband married her sister. If a woman's husband died, she married her husband's brother.

In the case of a death, there was open mourning. The deceased belongings were burned and part of their house was torn out and destroyed. If a band leader died, they might have chosen to move their camp.

The Bannock were Plains Indians. In the Plains style, the warriors wore breech clouts, leggings and moccasins. They painted their faces to go to war or on raids. They were armed with lance, bow and arrows or rifles. Bannock Indians counted coup, by stealing horses from their enemies. Since prehistoric times the Bannock were "hunters and gatherers." The Snake bands went from place to place gathering food in four rhythmic seasonal cycles. Bannock hunters targeted antelope, bear, buffalo, deer, mountain sheep, rabbit, and brought game back to the band. Smaller parties could ride on horseback to hunt antelope and deer.

As buffalo began disappearing from the base of the Blue Mountains, the Bannock crossed the Snake River to follow them. Bannock Indians migrated into the southeast corner of what became what is now Idaho from now Oregon and Nevada, and continued eastward to Fort Hall. Buffalo then grazed in numbers on the Snake River Plain. The buffalo soon vanished from the Fort Hall area, after 1840.

The Snakes first referred to the Bannock as the "Robber Indians," because they counted coup stealing Shoshoni horses. Later, the Bannock people came to in the vicinity of the Fort Hall Shoshoni. Eventually, Bannock and Shoshoni Indians began to marry. The bond became so strong that an alliance was formed between the Bruneau River and Boise River Shoshoni. They became as one people..

The walking Bannock obtained the horse soon after their Shoshoni brothers. The horse revolutionized the Bannock's world. Transportation changed the hunt and warfare. Horses provided mobility to areas of subsistence and speed to raid or race. A travois loaded with supplies, was dragged behind a horse.

During their yearly food cycle, the Bannock people joined in fishing along the Snake River or traded the Shoshoni's for fish. Extended Bannock Indian families banded together, left Fort Hall and moved down along the Snake River, below Shoshone Falls to follow the Chinook salmon. Schools of hundreds of salmon amassed there that had failed to climb the falls. The Bannock traveled westward toward the now Boise, Payette and Weiser Rivers continuing to fish. Indians fished there for several weeks, catching salmon. They dried the salmon for storage.

As the season changed, the Bannock families moved up in the hills to the Camas Prairie to dig the wild Camas root. The women also dug other roots and picked seeds. In the autumn they migrated south to pick the pinion pine-nut. The camas was also the "medicine camas, used for gynecology and during childbirth.

Groups of Bannock and the Nez Perce Indians would meet to dance and trade goods. The Nez Perce camped alongside of the Bannock and entered into the festivities and trade. Buffalo robes, horses, beads, wives and various goods were traded. The Bannock traded buffalo robes to the Nez Perce for skin war shirts. They danced in celebration. Teepees were placed in a large circle, a favored formation of camp teepees during celebrations. It was not unusual to see Bannock, Nez Perce and Shoshoni Indians joined in one encampment. Wealth was counted in Buffalo robes, horses and beaver pelts.

Sometimes, the Bannock Indians traded directly with mountain men and fur traders. Jim Bridger and Captain Benjamin L. Bonneville were two of the traders they bartered with. Rarely the Bannocks invited white men to hunt buffalo with them. They were excellent hunters and fierce warriors. They took Blackfoot scalps, showing much bravery.

hey expected any white person entering their camp to observe their customs
nd smoke the pipe with them. If the whites ignored these policies, the Bannock
ight turn on them and attack, being horse thieves, the Bannock were generally
disliked by white people and were described as fierce and warlike. Three
annock warriors captured Charles Ogden, from Fort Boise, and held him for
ree days. The warriors released him when they discovered he was British and
ot an American. Bannock Indians could be mean and were not afraid of the
hite man.

There had been numerous bison on the Snake River Plain westward
to Oregon to the base of the Blue Mountains before the turn of the Nineteenth
entury. The buffalo had disappeared after that due to over-kill. With a scarcity
f bison on the Snake River Plains, hunters had to travel to the Upper Missouri
find buffalo.

As autumn turned to "Indian Summer," a mixture of Bannock and
hoshoni Indians would ride to the Upper Missouri region and the Montana
ains. Bannock hunters, like the Shoshoni, formed a large group and departed
n the long excursion over the Great Bannock Trail, for their annual hunt. It was
e most important hunt of the year. Other Bannock Indians would accompany
e Lemhi Shoshoni or Eastern Shoshoni on the hunt.

The buffalo hunters left Fort Hall under direction of the war leader. The
ar leader might double as the hunt leader. They were careful to travel in as a
rge hunting party for their own safety, in case Blackfoot warriors were waiting
 ambush. They rode over land through Tahgee Pass and across the
ellowstone to Clark's Fork and continued over the Continental Divide to the
pper Missouri River in what is now, Montana. They followed the Bannock
rail.

The Shoshoni first described Bannock "as one who always steals horses
om me." Bannock considered stealing horses was an act of taking coup. The
annock Indians had the horse, early. When the Shoshoni rode to the upper
lissouri in now Montana they took the Bannock with them. The route to the
pper Missouri would become known as the "Bannock Trail." The trail was used
y the Bannock, Flathead, Kalispel, Kutenai, Nez Perce and Shoshoni buffalo
unters for decades. They returned with their pack horses laden with buffalo
eat and robes.

Raids were made on enemy bands to retrieve stolen horses. The
annock Indians were ready to fight any Blackfoot. They were strong warriors
nd not afraid to engage them in battle. Blackfoot warriors were a fierce foe, but
ey often found a Bannock war-party to be strong contenders. Skilled in
ghting, the Bannock warriors often had the victory. They did not hesitate to
alp their fallen enemies, counting coup in that manner. A victory dance or
alp dance was performed on their return from war. They collected a lot of
uns and acquired many scalps. Bannock Indians delighted in stealing horses
om other tribes, building up large herds. Wealth was measured in the number
f horses that they owned.

#16. The Bannock Indian People
(Courtesy of the Idaho State Historical Society)

Besides the Scalp Dance, the Bannock performed other dances. The Grass Dance was conducted by the head man in autumn. The Sun Dance was adopted late from the Plains culture. Social events were organized by the head man or band chief. The band chief usually had a crier give the news.

Bands joined together in the winter to form a village. Fort Hall Indians set up camp on the Snake River bottoms, above now, American Falls. In this way they could maintain the old way of living, as the band chief led forays to hunt for food. The Bannock people wintered with the Shoshoni on the Blackfoot River, Portneuf River and Snake River bottoms.

The Bannock that intermarried with the Shoshoni were more passive, but did not trust other bands. At times they seemed friendly, but would return and attack at a moment's notice. Some Bannock chiefs were actually friendly to the white man. Others distrusted them and attacked their wagons.

A Bannock chief's responsibility was to attempt to control his reckless young warriors. Donald McKenzie spoke with Bannock Chief Amaquen about murders of the white man by members of his tribe. The chief said that it was Banatee's (Bannock reengages) that had massacred the Reed party, in 1813. McKenzie, Ogden and Ross all had a dislike for the Banatee robbers and killers.

They wanted to make an example of them. The Bannock had stolen hundreds of traps. Trappers Beckwourth, Bridger and Ogden engaged the Bannock in battle if there was good reason to fight. Trappers usually maintained good relations with the Indians.

Fort Hall was a stockade fur fort built along the Snake River, in 1834 by Nathaniel Wyeth, 300 miles east of Fort Boise. Wyeth's luck was bad and he wound up selling the fur trade post to the Hudson's Bay Company. In a few short years the Hudson's Bay Company had trapped out the precious beaver.

In 1841, Jesuit Father De Smet arrived among the Bannock, accompanied by twenty Flathead Indians, led by "Little Chief." The treacherous Bannock had just finished smoking the "peace pipe" with the Flathead party, when they attacked them on their way back to camp. They had no honor. Nine of the attackers were killed. According to Father De Smet the Flatheads decided that it was the Sabbath and knelt to pray. The attack was over. The next day their chief promised the priest that he would try to influence his band to accept his teachings. Father De Smet tried to convert the Bannock Indians, baptizing them, as he had the Blackfoot, Flathead, Kutenai and Nez Perce Indians.

After 1842, as wagon trains came west. hundreds of white intruders merged on Indian land. They shot their game, took their water and pastures. The Bannock Indians were not fond of the white man and white people were mostly afraid of the Indians. Some just shot the Bannock on sight. Bannock Indians massacred the occupants of the John Reed cabin. Often, war parties were carried out by young reckless Bannock braves. Shoshoni braves joined them. They attacked the wagon trains again and again.

The Fort Hall Shoshoni Tribal Council did not approve of the raids. At times they clashed over the subject. The Bannock did not trust the "white eyes."

The Fort Hall Shoshoni were much friendlier toward them. Sometimes, when met on their own terms, the Bannock were friendly to the whites.

In 1848, Joe Meek traveled from Oregon Territory to Fort Boise en route to Fort Hall. He wore the Canadian Scotch plaid bonnet and red belt of the Hudson's Bay Company, hoping for safe passage through Bannock Country. Meek arrived at a Bannock Indian village, while warriors acted out, taunting him. Meek calmly, asked them to parley and explained that he was on official Hudson's Bay Company business. The Indians allowed him to continue to Fort Hall.

Mormon leader Brigham Young was governor of Utah Territory, in 1857. During the Utah War on September 11, 1857, emigrants with the Fancher-Baker wagon train, bound for California from Arkansas, were brutally massacred in Utah Territory.

Other trouble was brewing. It was rumored among the Mormons, that the gun that had killed Joseph Smith was on board that particular wagon train and that the territorial governor and ex-superintendent of Indian Affairs, Brigham Young, had incited the Bannock Indians to riot. The 300 Bannock Indians, joined by some 50 Mormons in Indian dress, waited to attack the emigrants.

Emotions ran high among them. At first, John D. Lee, a Mormon, dressed in Indian garb, felt remorse and attempted to prevent the killings. The Mormons and Indians brutally massacred one hundred and twenty innocent men, women and children. Seventeen kidnapped infants were taken to be raised by Mormon families. Their wagons, livestock and other possessions were divided and their clothes given to the Indians. The corpses would lie for two years on that killing field. Many of the bones were dragged off by scavengers before being interred in a mass grave.

Jewelry from those massacred was purposely given to Lee and used as evidence to convict him of the murders. Prosecution was put off for years. He was made the scapegoat. It was twenty years after the massacre, when Lee was tried. He disavowed the Mormon Church, as he was blindfolded and executed by firing squad. The Mormon Church apologized for the incident, much later.

The Nez Perce gambled with the Bannock, but the horse-thieves could not always be trusted. In 1857, Bannock warriors made numerous raids on the Nez Perce camps to steal horses. Sixty Nez Perce horses were stolen by the Bannock Indians. The two tribes nearly went to war over these incidents. The Nez Perce retaliated and set out to get their horses back. .

During the Utah War, the Bannock Indians began stealing horses and livestock from the Mormon ranchers. U.S. forces came to Utah to engage the Mormon militia in battle. A trader named John W. Powell incited the Bannock, by telling them the Mormons at Fort Lemhi were plotting to take their land. John Powell signed a sworn statement claiming that Brigham Young had tried to bribe the Bannock to join the Mormons in fighting the United States.

The Bannock refused Young's offer and decided, instead to join the war against the Utah settlers, who had sold munitions to the Nez Perce Indians, their enemies. This enabled the Nez Perce to steal horses, unopposed from the Bannock and Shoshoni Indians. The Mormon settlers consequently were run out of the Lemhi Valley. The Indian's reasoning was that Mormons had taken Indian land without paying for it. Taking revenge, the Bannock ran off Mormon livestock in retaliation. Bad feelings continued and emotion ran high. In 1857 the Snakes attacked Fort Lemhi, near the Salmon River. They justified the attack, reasoning that the United States had declared war on the Mormons.

A large village of 500 Bannock Indians camped near Fort Scot in Utah Territory. The Bannock chiefs were on good terms with the Army. One captain noticed that the Bannock west of Salt Lake seemed to be treacherous thieves, contrasting the two groups. Peace talks at Fort Scott were arranged with the Eastern Shoshoni leader, Chief Washakie. During the talks the Bannock chiefs remained silent. This surprised the officials, who knew that the Bannock and Shoshoni hunted the buffalo together.

Chief Washakie spoke for the Green and Wind River Shoshoni and Jim Bridger interpreted. Bridger said that he had traded with the Bannock for thirty years. He testified that when he had been introduced to the Bannock Indians, they had 1,200 lodges. Superintendent F. W. Lander, from Fort Kearney maintained that the settlers had destroyed pastures that the Indians had used to graze their horses. He thought it only fair that they receive monetary reparations for this.

On a visit to Fort Owen in 1858, it was noted, by Indian agent John Owen, that the Bannock had stolen 100 horses from Bitterroot Valley settlers. Owen held a council with the Indians when he returned to Fort Hall. Emigrants in eastern Idaho Territory were feeling the backlash of Bannock and Shoshoni Indian raiding parties. Indian marauders raided wagons, killed and wounded emigrants. The raiders tried to sell some of the stolen items in Utah territory. Superintendent Floyd requested that troops from Camp Floyd be sent to overtake them.

An Army company, under Major Isaac Lynde, was dispatched to Bear Valley in Idaho Territory to hunt for the Bannock. Meanwhile, Lt. E. Gay and troops left Camp Floyd to investigate the Goose Creek Massacre site. He learned that about 200 Bannock and Shoshoni Indians were encamped in Devil's Gate Canyon. Lt. Gay and a force of 42 recruits attacked them. After the battle, Gay counted only six wounded. An estimated twenty Bannock Indians were dead.

The same band was later reinforced in Cache Valley by around 300 Shoshoni, while a unit was sent to join Lt. Gay. They rode to join Major Lynde. They met where the Bear River crossed the Oregon Trail. On his way, Gay arrested Chief Pocatello. When they reached the post, Lynde released the chief for lack of evidence. Major Lynde said that it was not safe to antagonize the local Indians.

The Snake Indians were on the warpath in the Bannock country of eastern Idaho territory. Massacres were frequent during that period. It was decided that this was not a good time for emigrants to be moving west. Meanwhile, the Indian attacks on wagon trains continued. On August 16, 1859, the Lynde Post at Bear River received the report of an attack on a wagon train twenty miles east of the junction of Fort Hall and Hudspeth roads. Four emigrants had been killed. A number of Snake chiefs were responsible for the raid.

A Shoshoni band attacked an Army company led by Daniel Beal on Marsh Creek, killing one soldier. Nineteen men, women and children were attacked about dusk, twenty five miles west of Fort Hall. Eight people were killed, with some mutilated.

Bannock Indians became antagonized when their own people were being shot and killed by emigrants. Bear River country was a hot spot for Bannock attacks. The majority of the raids were made by the Bannock and fewer by Shoshoni Indians. Tensions between the emigrants and the Bannock reached high proportions. Emigrants on the wagon trains feared Indian attack The Army concentrated on ways to keep the attackers away from emigrant roads.

In the 1850's, the Hudson's Bay Company called Chief Oytes, a friend to the white man. Teverewera, "the long man" was chief of 600 Bannock Indians in the Humboldt basin. In 1860, Fort Boise Bannock Chief Poemacheah ("Hairy Man"), boasted 100 lodges in his village. They subsisted on buffalo meat, fish, roots, salmon and wild vegetables.

The Bannock Indians attained a reputation for stealing horses with other Indians and being hostile toward whites. They had plundered nearly every wagon train that crossed through their country. The Bannock Indians were described as the most warring and powerful tribe west of the Rocky Mountains. Bannock and some Shoshoni bands were constantly raided and attacked wagon trains.

James D. Doty, of the Utah Indian Affairs learned from Chief Little Soldier, an Indian informant, who said the Utah Bannock and Shoshoni Indians were determined to make a successful war on America. The two tribes made an alliance to eradicate all emigrants and settlers that passed through their country. To achieve this goal, they decided to exclude Chief Washakie (peace chief), and elect the Bannock Chief Pashego (man of blood), instead.

In Utah Territory, a group of Californians were attacked by Eastern Bannock. All but two people perished. The next month more emigrant trains were plundered by Indians. The Indians targeted every wagon train that passed through. Mormon settlements were constantly besieged by Bannock and Shoshoni thieves. Horses and stock were run off on a steady basis. The Oregon Trail was a hotspot and not safe for traveling homesteaders.

In 1860, two large groups of Bannock Indians roamed western Utah Territory. A southern group of Indians in 45 lodges was led by Chief Mopeah. The northern group was led by the great Chief Le Grande Coquin (Ar-ro-ka-kee), a famous Bannock horse thief named "Great Rogue" by French Canadian fur trappers. The chief bragged that they could attack any wagons leaving Fort Hall for Oregon and would tolerate no white eyes passing through their country.

In August of 1860, the Otter Massacre occurred. Forty-four emigrants in a wagon train traveled along the Snake River near Shoshone Falls, in Idaho erritory. They were ambushed by a band of Snake Indian warriors. Eighteen people were killed while four children were captured and two were lost in the mountains. Of those remaining, just 15 lived. Five that had died were eaten by the surviving 15, to keep from starving. During the ordeal, Major John Owen made an attempt to recover the children. A band of 60 Snakes attacked another wagon train near the City of Rocks, on September of 1860, in Idaho Territory. A patrol of soldiers arrived and broke up the fray, but the emigrants lost a lot of gear.

In 1861 the Civil War broke out between the northern and southern states. Gold was discovered in 1862 in the Boise Basin. Miners infringed on Indian land. They found gold on the Nez Perce Reservation and in the Black Hills. The gold-rush to Idaho City and Silver City along the Salmon River and Coeur d'Alene River opened up mining; thousands of miners moved into Idaho Territory. The tent city of Lewiston was named capital while Idaho City became a boom town with the largest population in the Pacific Northwest.

Prospectors led by George Grimes left Auburn, in Oregon Territory, mid-July of 1862. They employed some Snake Indians as guides to the Boise Basin. Six miles outside Bannock, (present day Idaho City) near Centerville, they discovered gold. The prospectors were ambushed by Bannock and Grimes was murdered.

The Bannock and Shoshoni warriors prepared for an all out war. They took their families to the Salmon River Mountains for their safety. Wargika, a Bannock prophet whom the Bannock and Shoshoni trusted, was in charge of the Indians' movement to the hills. Small Bannock war parties that first initiated raids now numbered nearly 300 warriors strong. The conditions for emigrants traveling west along the Oregon Trail were not good at this time. Signs were posted along the trail warning emigrants of the warring Bannock and Shoshoni raids.

Three wagon trains were massacred near Soda Springs, in Idaho Territory. All the emigrants were cut down. Two hundred horses were stolen from Fort Bridger by Snake Indian marauders. A chase followed by 62 volunteers who hoped to take back the stolen ponies, but only forty horses were recovered. A company of soldiers en route to the Salmon River Mountains lost five men to an Indian invasion. An Iowa company was stormed by Snake Indians and experienced seven loses on Sublette's Cutoff.

A party of eleven wagons that traveled west of American Falls, in Idaho Territory, was massacred by about a hundred Snake Indians. Nearly all the travelers were killed. The place is now a landmark, called Massacre Rocks. A larger wagon train arrived too late to help. The Indians had stolen wagons and livestock. The next day 40 armed settlers began to follow their trail and without warning, 300 mounted Indian warriors appeared. The group fled for their lives and only three of them were shot by the Indians. For safety, the emigrants began to amass a huge wagon train before proceeding on west.

McGarry intended to curtail the theft of horses and livestock. He and his troops left Salt Lake on December 10, 1862, to do just that. His mission was to recover some of the stock stolen from the settlers the previous fall. McGarry took four Indians captive and sent an Indian lad to the village. He was to relay to the villagers that unless the stolen stock was returned to them, the four Indians would be killed. The Shoshoni ignored the message and McGarry had the prisoners shot. This riled up the Indians. A Council was held. The Shoshoni vowed to avenge the deaths. Two dispatch carriers were gunned down shortly thereafter. True to their word, the Indians tried to kill every white man north of the Bear River.

January 3, 1863 ten miners en route to Salt Lake were killed by Indians. Three days later, eight more miners were attacked and John Smith was murdered. Because of the deaths, a fellow miner filed petition before Utah Chief Justice Kinney. A warrant was issued for the arrest of Chiefs Bear Hunter, Sagwitch and San Pitch. Marshall Gibbs, under Kinney's warrant, passed the order on to Colonel Patrick E. Conner, who had come to this region to solve the Indian problem.

During the Civil War, in 1863, President Abraham Lincoln ordered the Army west to deal with the Indian problems. Major Edward McGarry and two companies of enlisted men had been instructed to rescue a white boy, who had been captured by Chief Bear Hunter and his Shoshoni band of Indians. The Major and troops attacked Bear Hunter's camp, in Cache Valley at dawn. Three Indians were killed, while one brave and two women were captured. The rest retreated into the hills and a parley was called. The Army held Bear Hunter hostage until the boy was retrieved.

#17. "In the Shadows" Drawing by Len Sodenkamp, Boise artist

#18. The Bannock loved the buffalo hunt.
Sketch by Len Sodenkamp, eminent Boise artist

BATTLE OF BEAR RIVER

Colonel Conner stated that he planned to take no prisoners of those that resisted. His plan was to chastise the Utah Indians for their wrong-doings. Conner marched at night from Salt Lake, in order to provide the element of surprise. Two cavalry units marched at once, traveling at night. The town of Preston, Idaho had heard of the approaching troops.

Meanwhile, Chief Bear Hunter's Shoshoni warriors did a war dance around the home of Mormon Bishop Preston Thomas, demanding wheat. The next day, Bear Hunter returned and was told that the soldiers were near. Hearing that he could be killed, Bear Hunter stated that the soldiers might be killed, also. The chief rode to warn his people.

At dawn, on January 29, 1863, Colonel Conner and his two companies swam their horses across the icy cold Bear River, one mile south of Bear Hunter's encampment. The Indian camp was nestled in a ravine. A Shoshoni chief sat on his horse, with a human scalp dangling from a stick and touted them. The Indians harassed and shouted at them and when the soldiers were in range, the fighting began. The soldiers dismounted and returned fire. Conner sent the cavalry to aid the infantry. He had 200 men at his disposal.

Bear Hunter's Shoshoni had little avenue of escape; still about 100 warriors fled into the hills or across the river. The fighting was carried on for four hours. The Army estimated some 300 Indians were dead, while 160 survived. Chief Bear Hunter was killed while making bullets, in front of his campfire. Chiefs Pocatello and Sagwitch had left the previous day and were not present during the battle. Conner left some wheat for the survivors to eat. Women and children had also lost their lives, also. Many lay injured. It was not a pretty picture. The soldiers destroyed 70 teepees and captured 175 horses. They had found 1,000 bushels of wheat and plunder, stolen from the settlers.

A rumor reached Camp Douglas that Chief Pocatello and his Shoshoni warriors were seeking a fight with General Conner and his troops. Meanwhile, the Bannock Indians had moved into the Wind River Mountains.

General Conner had decided go to Fort Hall to remove any remaining hostiles. He left Salt Lake by nightfall with a large group of Cavalry. At the Snake River Ferry, he came upon 17 Shoshoni lodges. There body language was promising, so Conner gave out gifts to the Shoshoni. He told them that if they sought peace, they would not meet the fate of those at Bear River.

In 1863, the Bannock killed a white man near Brigham City. Rumor held him to be an emigrant. Chief Snag and two braves came in to town to answer the charge that they had held a white captive. The three Indians were shot down in the street at Bannock City by a group of miners. An emigrant wagon train was later attacked by Indians, 40 miles west of Fort Hall. Attacks on wagon trains slowed to a stop. Conner's near-massacre at Bear River had made an impression. The Indians chose to ignore the situation and left the area to hunt buffalo in Montana. Sentiment between the Indians and the settlers was not good, however.

In May of 1863 Chief Winnemucca promised Indian Agent John Burche of Nevada that he would intercede and persuade Chief Pashego (Pas-se-quah) of the Bannock of Nevada and Idaho to attend a conference. Burche met with the chiefs on the Humboldt River and Pashego promised that there would be no more attacks on the white man. To insure peace, the chief promised to keep his Bannock away from major routes. Pashego agreed, if the white man would leave the Indians alone.

Colonel Conner and a large force met with nearly 300 Shoshoni Indians (17 lodges) at the Snake River Ferry. He spoke of peace with them and gave out presents. He told them that peace was desired and that he did not want to have to repeat what had happened at Bear River. Chiefs Pocatello, Sagwitch and San Pitch were not with them, though.

August 21, 1867, Ballard met with Tah-gee. They talked of getting the reserve at Fort Hall. Governor Ballard spoke,

"Now, are you willing to relinquish your title to all of the country you have claimed provided the government of the United States secures to you and your children, and to such other friendly Indians as maybe induced to go thereon, the sole ownership of said reservation forever, supply you with subsistence until you can raise sufficient for yourselves and furnish you an agent, teachers, books, implements of husbandry, etc."

Chief Tah-gee answered, "I thought when the white people came to Soda Springs and built homes and put soldiers in them, it was to protect my people, but now they are all gone, and I do not know where to go, or what to do."

"The white people have come into my country, and have not asked my consent... And why have no persons talked to me before?...I have never killed white people who were passing through my country...All the Bannock will obey me and be good, but the Sheep-eaters are not my people and I cannot be responsible for them. I will answer for the Bannock...The buffalo do not come as far south now as formerly, so we go further to the north to hunt them. The white people have scared them away.

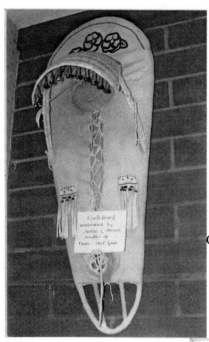

#19. Paiute Indian Cradle board - This cradleboard was handcrafted by Justine L. Brown, daughter of Paiute Chief Louie (Photo courtesy of Jackson Cramer)

#20. Bannock girl carries firewood. During the winter, Bannock girls stacked six piles of firewood daily. (Courtesy of the Idaho State Historical Society)

I am willing to go on the reservation, but I want the privilege of hunting e buffalo for a few years. When they are all gone far away we hunt no more; erhaps one year perhaps two or three years; then we stay on the reservation all e time... I want the right of way for my people to travel when going to or ming from buffalo country, and when to sell our furs and skins. I want the ght to camp and dig roots on Canyon Prairie when coming to Boise City to ade... I will go from here to the buffalo country, where I will meet my tribe, d will tell them of this talk and of the arrangements we make. I am willing to on the reservation as you propose. We can go next spring."

At the council Chief Washakie agreed that his Eastern Shoshoni would ove to the reservation. Chief Tah-gee spoke, and said he wanted a different servation for the Bannock. The Bannock were reluctant to go onto the servation. The Bannock were separate from the Shoshoni. They wanted special eatment.

THE FORT BRIDGER TREATY OF 1868

On July 3, 1868, Bannock Chief Tah-gee (Tag-gee) and 800 Bannock rived at Fort Bridger. Chief Tah-gee pushed to keep the Camas Prairie as part f the reservation. Army officers in charge were W.T. Sherman, N.G. Taylor, Lt. eneral William S. Harney, John B. Sanborn, S.F. Tappan, C.C. Augur and revet Major General Alfred H. Terry. The treaty of Fort Bridger, July 3, 1868, ade division between the Goshiute Shoshoni and the Wi-hin-asht Shoshoni of estern Idaho Territory. These were the Boise, Bruneau and Weiser River oshoni Indians. They were referred to as the Western Shoshoni Indians. almon-eater and the Sheep-eater Shoshoni were called the Northern Shoshoni dians. The treaty made provision for Shoshoni-Bannock Indian reservations. rt Bridger Treaty Council of 1868 met July third; the treaty was signed tween President Andrew Johnson of the United States of America and the oshoni-Eastern Band-and Bannock in the Territory of Utah.

The Treaty of Fort Bridger 1868 called for the arrest of any Bannock or oshoni fugitives. The treaty provided for a reservation for the Bannock when ey were ready or by the President. Buildings, including a school would be nstructed for Eastern Shoshoni and Bannock Indians. These Indians would ake their home on the reservation, and could continue to hunt buffalo. The dian agent would make his home on the reservation, and direct the affairs of e Bannock Indians. Heads of family would each receive 320 acres to farm. A rson over 18 years of age would receive 80 acres to farm. A person over 18 ars of age would receive $100 worth of seeds the first year and $25.00 per ar for the next three years. Compulsory education was required for children es 6-16 years old. The list of annuity goods would be payable on September 1, year for thirty years. It provided for a list agency employees, including a ysician. All treaties of reservation lands had to be voted on by a majority of e tribes. Gifts were given for the best farming operations for the first three ars. Annuities were paid yearly to the Indians at Fort Bridger.

General W.T Sherman and U.S. Army officers signed. A. Whit
Secretary attested to the treaty. Henry A. Morrow, (witness), Luther Manp
(Indian Agent), W.A. Carter, J. Van Allen Carter, (Interpreter), attended.

Shoshoni Indians signing were: Washakie, Waunypitz, Toopsepowo
Narkok, TaBoonshe, Bazeel, Pantoshega and Ninnybitse. Bannock India
signing: Tahgee, Taytoba, Weratzewonagen, Cooshagan, Pansookamotse a
Awite-etse. All of these Indians signed by making their mark. Bannock Chi
Tag-hee did all he could to get the Camas Prairie included as part of the
reservation. The Camas provided much of their food source. In 1869, land w
set aside for a Bannock Indian Reservation at Fort Hall, Idaho.

In August of 1868, the Bannock and Shoshoni bands were still campe
on the Boise River. The Indians were allowed to hunt buffalo in the previo
fall. The Bannock kept their word and were peaceable from the treaty in 1863
the second treaty in 1868. They had been friendly to the emigrants, the who
time.

In 1868, the Sioux Indians drove the Bannock and Shoshoni out
Yellowstone. In 1869, a fight with the Sioux left 29 Bannock and Shosho
dead. On April 13, 1869, Agent Powell led 850 Bruneau Shoshoni, 300 Boi
Shoshoni and 150 Bannock Indians from Boise to Fort Hall Indian Reservation

The Bannock Indians were hunting buffalo with the Eastern Shosho
in the Wind River Mountains. On their return, the Bannock stopped by Fort Ha
to receive their presents. When they were at the fort, Chief Tah-gee spoke wi
the agent and told him that they were ready to move to Fort Hall. The govern
was advised and he passed it on to the Indian Commissioner. By executi
order, President Grant on July 30, 1869, granted the Bannock Indians a home
Fort Hall Indian Reservation.

Various problems arose in managing Chief Tendoy's Shoshoni w
wouldn't come in to Fort Hall. They were jealous of the Bannock and the
presents. In 1870 the Shoshoni-Bannock fought Arapaho warriors. The Banno
struggled from 1870-1877, even though they hunted the buffalo.

#21. War-chief Buffalo Horn Led his
Warriors in the Bannock War of 1878.
(Courtesy of the Idaho State Historical Society)

On January 1871, a new agent, J.N. High recognized that if the Bannock didn't hunt the buffalo, they could not subsist. There were not enough rations to sustain them. He wrote the Commissioner of Indian Affairs in Washington about the problem. The hunters returned from the Plains with news that Chief Tah-gee had died during the winter. War-chief Pansookamotse (Otter Beard) became chief of the Bannock. Otter Beard died three years later. Chief Ty-hee became Chief of the Bannock Nation; his son succeeded him.

In 1872, a Crow Indian Agent deputized two white men. They arrested two Bannock Indians accused of stealing Crow Indian horses. One Bannock ran and was shot dead. In 1872, a Crow chief, named "Little Iron," killed a Flathead Indian. For revenge, some Crow friends of the Flathead who was killed threatened to kill two of Chief Little Iron's Bannock friends. The chief, in turn, threatened to kill the Crow Agent. The agent opened his shops and gave everyone involved presents, as a reward for sparing his life.

The Bannock were at war with the Nez Perce Indians in the winter of 1872. The Bannock got word of a Nez Perce attack on them at Fleishman Creek in Montana, so they hid in snow tunnels. When the Nez Perce rushed the empty lodges, the Bannock warriors began firing. One Nez Perce died, another was wounded.

The Nez Perce and the Bannock Indians were enemies. Buffalo Horn had served as Bannock scout for General George Crook in the Sioux War. He completed a dangerous mission for General Nelson A. Miles along the Yellowstone River, with a Crow scout, Le Forge and Buffalo Bill Cody. The Nez Perce War escalated on June 17, 1877. Major Green's three companies of Cavalry and twenty Bannock scouts, led by Buffalo Horn, rode out of Fort Boise to join General Howard's 7th Cavalry in the fight against the Nez Perce.

Jacob Meeks, and four Bannock chiefs returned 15 stolen horses, as a goodwill gesture on behalf of Conner. A military post was then raised at Soda Springs, to guard the California and Oregon Trails.

The superintendent of Indian Affairs provided eight beef cattle and 3,000 pounds of flour to destitute to the Bannock families, with the understanding that General Conner would meet with them for the peace treaty on July 20, 1863. Doty and Agent Mann signed a treaty on July 2, 1863, with Chief Washakie of the Eastern Shoshoni. They again signed a Treaty with Chief Pocatello and the Northern Shoshoni at Box Elder, on July 30, 1863. An annuity was promised for lands that had been destroyed.

The Ruby Valley Shoshoni signed a Treaty on October 1, 1863. The Twilla Valley Goshiute Shoshoni signed on October 12. The Bannock signed an agreement with General Conner and Superintendent Doty at Soda Springs. 150 mixed Bannock and Shoshoni Indians, under Bannock Chief Le Grand Coquin with Sub-chiefs, Tag-hee and Matigund, representing a tribe of 1,000 people. Conner promised them $5,000 in annuity for damaged lands. The Bannock Treaties provided that the tribe not molest emigrant trains along the California and Oregon Trails. The Bannock were to receive $3,000 worth of provisions, in return, and a portion of the lands were to be retained by them. The treaties later had to be revised and then agreed to by the tribe, which was scattered. The Bannock would not sign the new treaty, as it did not agree with the Fort Bridger Treaty of 1863. It remained a de facto agreement until 1868.

Idaho was formed in 1863. Governor Caleb Lyon held talks with the Boise Shoshoni and the Camas Prairie Bannock and Shoshoni Indians. Governor Lyon was

the ex-officio Superintendent of Indian Affairs. A reservation was provided for those Bannock and Shoshoni Indians on the Snake River.

The five treaties negotiated in 1863, with the Bannock and Shoshoni Indians were confirmed by the U.S. Senate, with minor changes. It was necessary to discuss this with the five bands involved who signed. The Eastern Shoshoni agreed, along with the other Shoshoni groups. The Soda Springs Treaty was ratified by the U.S. Senate, but the Bannocks would not sign, since it differed from the Fort Bridger Treaty of 1863.

It took a long, slow process to get the Fort Hall Reservation established. 800 of Chief Tah-gee's Bannock Indians were under the control of the Indian Office, under the Treaty of Soda Springs. The Bannock Indians arrived at Fort Bridger, in the summer of 1884 and again in 1885 for the presents promised in the treaty. Both times, the Bannock went to hunt buffalo, instead. Agent Mann had trouble receiving an annuity for the Bannock, while Washakie's Eastern Shoshoni received all $10,000 worth. Mann even dug into his own pocket to pay them, himself. He wrote to the Secretary of the Interior in behalf of the Bannock.

Agent Powell was instructed on July of 1866 to take responsibility for the Boise River and Bruneau River Shoshoni bands also, one band of Bannock that were camped near Boise City. Powell moved them 30 miles to a location on a fork of the Boise River. The Bannock chief in charge was Chief Bannock John. Agent Powell said the actual count was 283 Boise Shoshoni, 300 Bruneau Shoshoni and 100 Bannock.

Bannock
Braves"
MaJor
Moorhouse

22. Bannock Warriors-
(Courtesy of the Idaho State Historical Society)

Governor Lyon signed a treaty in 1866, on which the Bannock agreed go onto a reservation. It was never ratified, but Governor Ballard, the new governor, learned that 400 Bruneau Shoshoni agreed that they and the Camas Bannock and Shoshoni were eager to go onto the reservation.

At that time, $25.00 to $100 was offered at public meetings for an Indian scalp. It was not safe for peaceable Indians to be out and about.

On June 1867, Indian leaders had a military escort to Boise for an interview with Governor Ballard. John and Jim Bannock were brothers that married Chief Tah-gee's two sisters. Tah-gee became chief of the Bannock nation, when Le Grand Coquin died. The two brothers represented the Indian tribes to the governor. Governor Ballard set aside Fort Hall in eastern Idaho, north of Pocatello, as the Indian reservation for the Boise, Bruneau Shoshoni and Bannock Indians, a total of 1,800,000 acres President Andrew Jackson issued an executive order establishing Fort Hall reservation, June 14, 1867.

THE BANNOCK WAR

The Bannock were generally peaceable on the Fort Hall Reservation. Never-the-less, the Bannock was reputed as fierce, warring Indians. They cherished the country in Montana, where they could hunt buffalo. The Bannock loved their Camas Prairie, where their women could dig the camas roots and gather other foods, and claimed this as their own land.

In 1878, Chief Buffalo Horn and the Bannock became angered when some settlers brought their hogs to the Camas Prairie to graze. Incidentally, the hogs did considerable damage to their land. This incident caused the Indians to rise up. Buffalo Horn's Bannock Indians visited the camp of the white men. They injured one man and threatened another, because of broken treaties. Buffalo Horn prepared for war, while Chief Tendoy's band chose peace and rode to the Lemhi River Reservation.

Buffalo Horn and 200 Bannock went to war. They attacked cattlemen in the Camas Prairie, killing two. A third man lived by hiding in the brush. Another fled on horseback to spread the word of attack to Fort Boise. He contacted a Captain Bernard. The marauders plundered wagons near King Hill. They stole arms, and fled across the Snake River using the ferry. Reaching the other side, they cut it loose. The Bannock killed some settlers at the mouth of the Bruneau River. Captain Egan along with some 46 Bannock and Weiser Indians joined Buffalo Horn. His band increased to 300.

Bernard's column pursued Buffalo Horn over the divide to the headwaters of the Owyhee River. Twenty volunteers, stationed at Silver City, reached the hostiles first and engaged them. They met with heavy fire. The volunteers retreated in a running battle. Chief Buffalo Horn was supposedly killed in the siege. It was rumored that he had escaped to Wyoming.

Egan replaced Buffalo Horn as leader. Their numbers grew to 800, as more joined them. Bernard and his men were outnumbered three to one. General Howard, known as the "one armed general," left Fort Walla-Walla for Boise

June 9, 1878. By June 18th, he had raised 900 troops, six officers and artillery handle the outbreak. (Howard lost his right arm by amputation. His arm wa shattered by a rebel "Minnie ball" while fighting in the Civil War). Bernard an several other excellent officers joined Howard's columns.

The marauders meantime rode toward the John Day River, in Orego Territory, killing ranchers and stealing their livestock. They proceeded along th Grand River into the Blue Mountains. The hostiles were now made up Malheur, Northern Paiute, Shoshoni, Umatilla, and Weiser Indians. Th Bannock continued their rampage. On the move, they covered hundreds miles. The Cavalry purposely
kept the renegades on the run. The rebels fought whenever the Cavalry overtoc them.

Captain Egan crossed the Columbia River offering the Umatilla India 2,000 horses to join them in battle. When they refused, the rebels opened fire them. At first, they fled. The Umatilla's returned, acting like they had change their minds suddenly the Umatilla opened fire and killed Captain Egan. Wi both Chiefs Buffalo Horn and Egan dead, the hostiles scattered, some still on th rampage. Others crossed into Idaho Territory attacking whites on the Salmo River and Payette Lake, moving into Montana.

U.S. Colonel Nelson A. Miles engaged the renegade Bannock, in 187 In an early morning raid, Miles, with 75 Cavalry plus Crow Indian scou managed a surprise attack on the hostiles killing eleven. This attack ended th Bannock War. Miles was l promoted to General, as Commander-in Chief of th U.S. Army, in 1895.

Rebel captives were taken from Fort Omaha and Fort Hall to Fc Simcoe, where Captain W. H. Winter delivered 600. Some were picked up alor the Columbia River by armed riverboats. Fugitives were jailed or returned to th reservation. In the Bannock War, nine soldiers died, twenty-four were wounde and twenty-four citizens were killed. Thirty-four were wounded. Seventy-eig Indians died. Sixty-six were injured.

23. Sergeant Jim Bannock Warrior
(Courtesy of the Idaho State Historical Society)

THE RESERVATION

The Bannock Indian Tribe united early with the Shoshoni Indians through intermarriage, becoming as one tribe. When it became time to go onto the reservation, the Bannock Indians joined the Shoshoni at Fort Hall, in 1869. Fort Hall was established by the Fort Bridger Treaty of 1868. 1.8 million acres were set aside for the four Shoshoni bands and one band of Northern Paiute, the Bannock Indians, at Fort Hall. The size of the reservation was reduced between 1868 and 1932 to 540,000 acres. Fort Hall is divided into five districts: Fort Hall, Lincoln Creek, Ross Fork, Gibson and Bannock Creek. Reservation land is 96% tribal and individually Indian owned. 70% of the 5300 tribal members live on the reservation. The Tribe employs nearly 1,000 native and non-native people in tribal government, enterprise and gaming. Their combined payroll is $30,000,000 and their goal is to build their economy and preserve the land- base for generations.

Chapter Three
NORTHERN PAIUTE INDIANS

The Southern Paiute resided in northwestern Arizona, southeastern California, southern Nevada and southern Utah. Southern Paiutes called themselves the "Nuwuvi or "the people." The Spanish made contact with these Paiute Indians. They called them," Payuchis." The Northern Paiute were called the Paviotso or Pahvant. They called themselves Numa or Numu, which translates, "the people." Pah, in their language means water and Ute means, "this way." The word Paiute is translated, "True Ute" or 'Water Ute."

The Northern Paiute Indians belong to the Uto-Aztecan family of Native American language group and spoke a different dialect not closely related to the Southern Paiute. The Bannock, Kawaiisu, Mono and Timbisha were Paiute Indian Numic speakers with different dialects, also. Bannock were closely related to Northern Paiutes, like the Mono people. The Kawaiisu favored the Southern Paiutes. The Timbisha more resembled the Shoshoni.

The various peoples that neighbored each other over the Great Basin spoke different dialects of the Shoshonean language group. The Northern Paiute bordered the Goshiute, (cattail eaters), Shoshoni, Northern Shoshoni, Southern Paiute and Ute Indians, all Uto-Aztecan speakers. Indians were normally at peace with each other and could co-habit in the same territory. The Northern Paiute Indians had the horse in the 1700's.

As was their custom, Paiute bands were composed of extended families numbering three or four generations. Camps or small villages helped provide solidarity in the extended family or families. A few non related families may have banded together forming a composite band.

The Northern Paiute Indians were semi-nomadic people that ranged across the Great Basin in what became east-central California, western Nevada and eastern Oregon. They dwelled in the Owens Valley and Surprise Valley regions of California, Pyramid Lake and Walker Lake and on the Humboldt and Truckee Rivers in Nevada and extended northward into eastern Oregon. The Northern Paiute Indians occupied the high desert region west of the Shoshoni Indians (in what is now, Oregon) and migrated into the riverine regions of western Idaho.

The Great Basin lies between the Rockies and the Sierra Mountain Range and forms a natural bowl, surrounded by mountains. After the Ice Age a giant lake formed from melting glaciers. After thousands of years the water dissipated. Creeks are few in numbers because of the arid climate and the lack of rainfall. Those usually ran into the lakes. The fresh water lakes evaporated and became salty.

#24. Roland Hanks, of Owyhee, Nevada
"Shoshoni-Paiute Powwow Dancer"
(Author Photo)

The Northern Paiutes learned to adapt to the ecology of the Great Basin. The winters were intensely cold. They endured summers of immense heat. It was a hard way of survival. The semi-desert country was sand, rock and sagebrush. In that environment, living on a creek, river or lake was necessary for their survival. Bathing, cooking and drinking was a must for them. They thrived on the flora and fauna from these regions. The life-way of the Northern Paiute was adaptation to the rugged desert element.

There was a division among the sexes, as there was among most great Basin tribes. Men hunted and fished. Women gathered. There was a strong work ethic among the Paiute. Girls began early helping their mothers glean berries, nuts and seeds. The boys went with their fathers, where they learned to fish and hunt early. Women caught small game and dug a variety of edible roots. Paiute women nurtured the plants they picked from, so that they would bear fruit again. Another important duty of the older daughters was to gather much needed firewood for cooking and warmth. Sometimes the children helped in this chore. Girls' duties were to pile five stacks of wood per day for cooking and heat when needed. Women handcrafted beautiful baskets, blankets, and clothing. Baskets were utilized to gather berries, nuts, roots and seeds. They were used to catch and carry fish. Baskets stored served as containers for foods in winter.

The Paiute migrated seasonally to hunt and gather food. The women gathered berries, fleshy parts, pine nuts, roots and seeds. At the same time, the men hunted fowl, game and fished. Foods were stored in underground pits for winter. Paiute women prepared meals for the family and cared for the children. In the early spring, the Paiute women began picking seeds. Females toted a large carrying basket, supported by a head-strap for weight, to contain seeds. They wore caps to protect their foreheads. The Northern Paiute had to adapt to the climate and found food by migrating from place to place. Euro-Americans combined the Bannock, Northern Paiute and Northern Shoshoni into one group. All three tribes were called Snake Indians or "Diggers," because of their root digging. Berries, dried fish, roots, seeds and grasses sustained them through the winter. They literally lived off of the land using every available resource possible.

During Indian summer (autumn) they traveled to the groves of pinion pine where they could harvest the pine nuts. Before moving up the slopes into the mountains for the harvest, the Paiutes held a powwow in celebration of the pine nut season and life. The festivities included dancing, singing and storytelling. They celebrated with a ritual prayer dance through the night, dancing shoulder to shoulder in a big circle, praying and singing songs about the animals, clouds and wind. The three festivals that were held annually were the Fish festival, pine-nut festival and Rabbit festival.

#25. Small Antelope Herd-The antelope made a good meal for the Paiute band. (Author Photo)

#26. Jack Rabbit-It took a number of rabbit pelts, sewn together for the Paiute to make blankets, clothing and robes. (Author photo)

The Paiute filled their water jugs when they moved up the mountain slope and reached a stream. Baskets lined with pitch were also filled with water before the Paiute climbed up to the pine groves. The pine nut was gleaned from the cone of the pinion pine, a scrubby coniferous tree found in the mountains of the Great Basin. It took a large quantity of the nuts. The men dislodged the cones by knocking them off of the pinion trees with long poles. The women and children gathered them in large baskets.

The pine cones were winnowed and dried in the sun. The pine nuts were roasted in a pit with embers covered with earth and pine boughs, overnight. Excess pine nuts were either stored in the ground for winter or ground into flour in mortar and pestles. The roasted nuts were stored underground in baskets, in skin-lined cedar boxes. They were removed in small portions for eating in late fall and winter. Pine nuts were ground in mortar and pestles into flour used to bake delicious and nourishing nut bread. Tiny pine nuts were good fresh, eaten off of the tree. Nuts were harvested from grove to grove.

The Paiute were superstitious. If they took food from the earth, they gave something back. When they picked berries or seeds, an object or a stone was left in its place. The elderly Paiute believed the owls would carry bad little children away in baskets. When a person died, the clothes were burned to keep his spirit from returning to claim them.

Game seemed to be more plentiful farther north in the Great Basin with more rainfall. The Paiute there hunted antelope, badgers, coyotes, ducks, foxes, jack rabbits, rattlesnakes and sage hen, when they could locate them. Deer were sometimes driven off of cliffs, similar to Shoshoni buffalo jumps. One method of hunting deer was the communal hunt. The deer were surrounded and shot with bow and arrows. A deer festival followed the hunt.

The Owens Valley Paiute of California Territory camped in the pinion groves and harvested them all winter. Game was hunted to facilitate the diet. Surprise Valley Paiutes in California Territory set traps for fowl and small game. Deep pits were dug and covered with pine boughs, in order to trap deer and other big game. They shot some game with bow and arrows. Game was scarce in this arid desert region and the Paiutes struggled for their existence. At times, they were forced to live from the lower end of the food chain, which consisted of ants, berries, birds, crickets, grasshoppers, insects, lizards, nuts, rodents, roots, seeds and snakes. Small burrowing animals were skewered with long sharp sticks.

In what is now western Idaho, the Northern Paiute celebrated the end of the fishing season in the fall with dance and celebration. The Paiute men used fishing camps to harvest fish for weeks at a time. Bow and arrows, nets, spears and harpoons were used to fish. A unique method of fishing was using a weed that contained a drug. Fishermen cut up the weed into small pieces and threw them into the water. The fish became intoxicated and swam to the surface and were caught. Women, assisted by their children, collected the fish. Pine nuts, rabbit and fish were at the top of their food chain.

Communal drives were used to entrap antelope, buffalo, deer, rabbit, sage hen, grasshoppers and crickets. Drives were an effective method to capture prey, involving the whole community. Drives for antelope were a communal activity. Herds of antelope could range into dozens. The antelope's defense from predators is being able to run in an instant at great speed and escape. The fur of the antelope was prized. The soft fur was used to clothe Indian babies.

In smaller communal antelope drives, the Indians circled the ruminants, and moved inward until the animal was ensnared. Antelope meat fed the whole band. Over a larger area, a communal antelope drive might have gone thusly. The Indians would spread out over a great distance in a huge circle and completely surround the herd. Then, they drove the antelope down lanes of brush and rocks into the catching corral. The Paiutes slaughtered what they needed and freed the remainder.

A different way of hunting the antelope, involved a medicine man. He would orchestrate the hunt. He used his wizardry to guarantee a good hunt. Antelope corrals were built. The shaman fashioned an antelope decoy of reeds. He played a crude musical instrument that emitted a screeching sound, evoking the antelope's curiosity. The Shaman chanted songs that were supposed to draw the antelope into the corral. Success on the hunt was attributed to the medicine man's magic. The next day if no antelope were in the trap, the Indians circled the herd and drove them into the corral. They were shot with arrows.

There were other ways to hunt antelope, involving a shaman. Shaman used his magic to entice the pronghorn, by his trickery and lure the antelope to come to him. He hid in the sagebrush and held a bright colored cloth tied to a long stick, high in the air. As the shaman slowly waved the flag back and forth, the curious antelope approached him and was easily shot with bow and arrows. Meat was shared by the band. An Antelope Festival followed the hunt with much festivity and dancing.

The Northern Paiute held communal grasshopper drives to gather grasshoppers and Mormon crickets for food. The band formed a huge circle around a host of grasshoppers and closed in on the insects and, ensnared them in nets in the center. Being rich in protein, the grasshoppers were pounded in a mortar into pulp, roasted on a stick and eaten or ground into flour for bread.

Rabbit drives were held during autumn. It was a communal activity, with several Paiute bands attending. Netting was stretched around desert bushes in a half-circle. The Indians surrounded the rabbits and then closed in on the rabbits. The netting provided an entrapment to catch the rabbits. The drive, also served as a social event. A festival was held following the hunt. The Paiute sang songs. Stories were told and games played. Young lovers courted. Festivities were enjoyed by all.

Communal drives were also used for the sage hen. Sage hen is another name for a prairie chicken or sage grouse. They are good eating. The Paiute community would surround the hens in a huge circle. They would then beat the ground with clubs and give war whoops, closing in on the hens. The sage hen (called fool hens) would fly, and then land a short distance ahead. The fool hens never flew far or high enough to escape, but were entangled in net snares in the center.

Rafts of woven tule reeds were constructed into a boat. Tule reeds were tied into two bundles and lashed together to create rafts. These boats were used to collect goose and mud hen eggs and also drive the waterfowl to shore, where they used sticks to club them. Sometimes netting was used to ensnare ducks or geese. The raft was propelled using long poles through the marshes.

The desert terrain was covered with sagebrush. The sagebrush was used for kindling. seeds and clothing. Tiny sagebrush seeds were eaten raw or could be made into a tea. In the absence of game, women made skirts of sagebrush. The bark was moistened and pounded in mortar and pestles, until stringy. The fibers were woven into cloth skirts. Sandals and garments were fashioned of sage brush fibers

During summer weather, the Indians wore scanty clothing in the summer. It was not uncommon for Paiute women to be nude from the waist up. During the summer, children ran naked until possibly around age six.

Clothing was often made of deerskin. The men wore deerskin breechclouts and moccasins. They wore Plains-type war-shirts, leggings and moccasins of deerskin in spring and fall. Men wore deerskin shirts and pants with their moccasins in the winter time. Women's clothing was also made of deerskin. In cooler weather deerskin dresses, leggings, and moccasins made up the females ensemble. A skirt with deer hoof rattles sewn on the fringe and moccasins were worn in the summer. Rabbit skins were utilized to make clothing. Rabbit skin robes were worn for warmth in the winter cold. Their fur was useful. It took about 200 rabbit skins to make a rabbit fur blanket or robe. The blankets made a warm, cozy blanket for sleeping in the wintertime. Baby clothing was made of soft animal fur.

Women wore beautifully woven conical basket hats to embellish and protect the head. The men also wore woven hats of basketry, which were more bowl shaped and shielded the scalp from the sun's rays.
Deer hooves, hollow bird bones and rabbit toes made earrings worn by both the men and women. Clam shells, which were bartered from the Pacific Coast Indians, made excellent earrings. Body piercings were common as were ear plugs and lip plugs. Colored clay was rubbed on the face and skin for adornment. Women wore intricate chin tattoos on their faces.

Stone amulets were fashioned, drilled and worn on necklaces. Necklaces and bracelets were popular. Indian jewelry was made of natural materials. Braids were often worn in the hair, adorned with otter fur interlaced and tied with leather strips. The Amerindian manufactured beads of bone, horn, and shell, stone and wood for centuries and commerce was lucrative among the Indian natives. Before the arrival of the white man, the Shoshoni had their own trade centers as did the Cheyenne, Crow, Mandan and Nez Perce. American traders introduced glass trade beads to them. Trade routes crisscrossed the Pacific Northwest.

Temporary houses could be erected in fishing and hunting areas. One type of house was a brush hut. This conical structure was covered with brush. A type of sleeping lean-to was hastily constructed between two bushes, with brush over the top. Another temporary shelter was constructed by the Paiute women. They piled brush into a circle, shoulder high, as a wind break.

Brush huts provided shade in the desert heat. A conical teepee frame or dome hut was constructed with saplings secured into the ground. Brush matting or thatch was tied together with sinew or strips of green bark. These were attached in layers as a covering. There was a door opening that could be closed for privacy.

Cattail teepees were a conical structure, covered with cattail sewn together into mats. These teepees had a small hollow in the earthen floor for a hearth. The Paiute women gathered the reeds by wading into the bogs to pull the cattails.

The Pit house was a permanent house suitable for winter. It was circular and excavated a few feet below ground level. It contained a cooking hearth, which also provided heat. It was cool in summer and warm in the winter.

The communal sweat lodge provided a social event for the male Paiutes, having a log framework. The structure was first covered with brush or woven mats and overlaid with a four to six inch layer of earth, with fire in an earthen pit in the floor. Water at times was added to create steam. The entryway was closed and an opening in the roof vented the steam.

The men would purge themselves in the steam for long period. Afterwards, they would run down and plunge themselves into an ice cold lake. This afforded them the best of health.

According to tradition birthing huts and menstrual huts were provided, which were constructed on the edge of camp for isolation. There was a cleansing that the young women did before entering, which was a type of religious ceremony.

CHIEF WINNEMUCCA

Chief Winnemucca was the great chief of the entire Northern Paiute Nation. There is a folk story about old Chief Winnemucca. The old chief was seen by trappers along the Humboldt River. He was wearing only one moccasin. His people began to call him "One Moccasin." In the Paiute language winni, was translated, (one) and mucca meant (moccasin), or Winnemucca.

#27. Old Chief Winnemucca-
One Moccasin." He was also called Truckee. His son was Chief Winnemucca
II. Old Winnemucca's granddaughter was Sarah Winnemucca. (Photograph
Courtesy of the Nevada State Historical Society)

Old Chief Winnemucca came into town nearly naked. Winnemucca was given an army uniform and hat, which he liked and wore. When Lieutenant John Fremont met the chief, it became a comedy of errors. Lieutenant Freemont asked "Old Winnemucca" a question. He would answer, "truckee, truckee," which in the Paiute language meant, "all right." Freemont assumed that his name was Truckee and recorded it that way. The name stuck and Chief Winnemucca became known as Chief Truckee. Winnemucca scouted for Freemont during the Mexican War.

In 1841 Colonel John Bartleson and John Bidwell led an emigrant party wagon-train from St. Louis heading to Fort Hall, southwest through Snake Country along the Humboldt River, through what is now Nevada, over the mountains into California. They told strange tales about a party of curious Snake Indians who followed them for some time, but did not attack them.

Sarah Winnemucca, the chief's granddaughter, told a humorous tale of her grandfather going out to meet the first white men in his territory. When white men appeared in the region that is now Nevada, they were the first white the Paiute had ever seen. Indians came to old Chief Winnemucca they told him of white men with beards that made camp in their vicinity. Winnemucca was happy and spoke, "My white brothers, my long looked-for white brothers have come at last!" The old chief took some of his trusted sub-chiefs and rode out their camp, expecting to greet them with open arms.

When the party of Paiutes arrived, the Euro-Americans were fearful and halted them. There was no interpreter. They used hand motions. There was no real communication. Chief Winnemucca acted out and threw down his robe demonstrating that he was unarmed and meant no harm. Still, the white men prevented their advance. Winnemucca was disappointed that they did not greet him but continued to follow. Each night as they camped, the Paiute camped near them, escorting the party for several days. The chief had been so anxious to meet them. Finally, Winnemucca turned his party around and they returned to the lodges. As the wagons rolled out of sight the emigrants thought they had escaped with their lives. Winnemucca returned home, saddened by the whole affair. This most likely was the Bartleson & Bidwell emigrant party, described earlier.

Chief Truckee was also called, "Captain Truckee." Captain Truckee later accompanied a party of white men traveling over the mountains California Territory in 1844.

Winnemucca II of the Nevada Northern Paiutes was the son of Old Chief Winnemucca, born around 1820 and commonly known as Poito. Chief Winnemucca was chief of the entire Northern Paiute Indian Nation, like his father before him. This included the Carson, Humboldt and Walker River Paiutes.

Some emigrants were so paranoid of Indians that they would shoot them on sight. This caused the Paiutes to fear the pioneers traveling west. During the great "California Gold Rush of 1849," prospectors began encroaching on Paiute lands.

When Silver was discovered in Nevada Territory the Paiute woes increased. Prospectors in Silver City, Gold City and Virginia City all had silver-strikes. Thousands of miners moved into the area. The miners cut the Paiute's pinion pines to build mine shacks. The mules grazed on plants and grasses, the seeds normally eaten by the Indians. Cyanide from the silver mines leaked into their streams, killing the fish. The white man drove the game off. Miners stole Paiute's horses. The Indians countered, stealing back cows and horses. They were forced to take jobs in town to live and were often mistreated.

THE PYRAMID LAKE WAR

Chief Winnemucca II was less trusting of the white man than his father, Chief Truckee. Yet he tried to keep the peace. The Pyramid Lake War of 1860 was provoked by a dishonest Indian Agent, who held back food, money and seed from the Paiutes. The Agent had shorted the Paiute people of rations at Fort McDermott and Pyramid Lake for some time. Two Paiute maidens were digging roots, when they were kidnapped. Natchez and more Paiutes scoured the countryside. They rescued the two girls that they found, bound and gagged in a cellar outside of Carson City, causing a Paiute uprising. A council was called for all the Northern Paiute Indians at Pyramid Lake. While they were in council, two white men were killed at William's Station. They decided on war and Chief Winnemucca was a proponent.

Army Major Ormsby and about 100 men searched for the Paiute band in order to punish them, following their tracks along the Truckee River for about 100 miles. On May 13, 1860, the Paiute War between Northern Paiutes, some Bannock and Shoshoni and the white settlers was fought in a meadow near Pyramid Lake. Chief Winnemucca formed his 600 warriors in a semi-circle on a low hill. The fighting was heavy, but Natchez Winnemucca saw that Major Ormsby was in trouble and rode to help his friend. It was too late. A brave rode in and shot him before the Major could be reached. 70 settlers were killed and only 25 Indians.

After the battle, U.S. soldiers were dispatched from California. This time, the Paiute were outnumbered and retreated into the mountains. The warriors remained with their families in safety. Fort Churchill was established in 1860 to protect the Pony Express Riders and settlers. Land was designated at Pyramid Lake for a reservation. Col. Frederick Lander set up a meeting with Chief Winnemucca.

#28. Sarah Winnemucca was the daughter of a Northern Paiute Indian chief in western Nevada. She was the champion of her people during the Bannock War. In later years she became an orator and author working for the cause of the Paiutes. Sarah was honored and made a chief.

(Courtesy of the Nevada State Historical Society)

The Colonel promised them the Pyramid Lake Reservation and also, that they would be taught to farm. Winnemucca was in agreement, but the Army reneged. The reserve land was leased to settlers and ranchers. Supplies came late and the Indian agent stole the shipments. He started his own store and sold the food and clothing back to the Indians, making them pay for their own supplies. No one taught them to farm and because of the conditions, they left the reservation. Many faced starvation and died, including Winnemucca's wife. Some worked in town. Others fished and hunted. Others looted and stole as repayment for their treatment.

SARAH WINNEMUCCA

In 1844, Winnemucca's wife, Tuboitone, gave birth to a baby daughter named "Shell Flower," for the pink hued desert flower. When Shell Flower became of age, she changed her name to Sarah. Sarah Winnemucca was the daughter of chiefs.

In 1850, when Sarah was six, her Grandfather Winnemucca had taken Sarah and her mother to visit a ranch in California, south of Stockton. When she was 16, her grandfather grew ill. His last wish expressed to his son was that Sarah and her siblings attend the mission school he had seen in San Jose. He died in 1860.

Winnemucca II had sent Sarah, her sisters and brothers to the mission school, but it lasted only a short time. The student's wealthy parents objected to Indians being there. Instead, Winnemucca sent Sarah to Mormon Station. She lived with Major and Mrs. William Ormsby and continued her education. Sarah left there to work in Virginia City as a maid, in order to buy books and continue to study.

After working as a servant in Virginia City, Sarah quit to take up the peoples' cause and urged her father to meet with the governor of Nevada Territory. Chief Winnemucca pleaded with the Nevada governor to stop the Indian agent from leasing their land to other white men. He requested that settlers not be allowed to be on their reservation. The governor pledged his support, but quickly forgot his promises. Conditions at Pyramid Lake remained the same and fighting resumed, with Indians stealing to eat.

Chief Winnemucca and the men from his Paiute band were on a fishing trip, when soldiers came and massacred 32 old men, women and children. Winnemucca's youngest son was killed. His daughter hastily mounted a horse and rode for her life to safety.

Chief Winnemucca took part of his Paiute band and departed for Oregon Territory, leaving his son, Natchez in charge of Pyramid Lake Reservation. Chief Natchez did not have much say. The reservation purse strings were held by the crooked Indian agent, Newgent. There was a plot to kill him, but Sarah warned Newgent about the plot. He and the settlers went to Fort

McDermott to expose the new plot. Smaller raids followed, but finally peace was reached in August of 1860, without a treaty.

Sarah and Natchez met with the commander of Fort McDermott, Col. James N. McElroy at Pyramid Lake. The colonel was a kind man. Sarah spoke for the Paiutes. She explained the plight of her people to him. He empathized with her and sent rations to the Indians with soldiers to guard them. He later brought the Paiutes to Fort McDermott and hired Sarah as his interpreter. Natchez rode out and rounded up stray Paiutes and brought them back with him.

Colonel McElroy was concerned about Chief Winnemucca. Natchez rode into Oregon Territory to find his father. Using an old Indian trick, he lit signal fires on various mountain tops. Natchez soon located the chief. Chief Winnemucca and his band returned to Fort McDermott with his son. The Indians were given large canvas tents to live in. Every day they received fresh meat and bread. They worked to earn a living there. They built homes, fences and fed cattle. The women had jobs and the men could leave the fort to hunt. They also harvested the pine nuts. Life at Fort McDermott was good for them.

Sarah was courted by several of the young army officers. One in particular, Lt. Bartlett took her to dances and horseback riding. When Bartlett received papers transferring him to Salt Lake, the young lovers eloped and married January 29, 1871. Chief Winnemucca opposed the marriage and it was doomed from the start. Bartlett was a drunk and Sarah didn't like city life. The chief sent an order for her to come home. So she and her brother Natchez returned to the fort.

When Colonel McElroy was transferred, the new post commander cut off their rations. The Paiutes drifted off of the fort and wound up at the Pyramid Lake Reservation. The new agent replacing Newgent was not much better. Sarah left Pyramid Lake to join her father in Oregon Territory.

While living at her father's camp, Sarah received a letter requesting her to fill the position as interpreter at the new Malheur reservation, established in 1872. Sarah rode with her father and brother to the reservation. The new agent, Sam Parrish was a decent sort. He gave out food and clothes rations regularly. He gave every Paiute a plot to farm and taught them farming. He furnished hay for the horses, plows and seed to plant, The Indians were industrious. They built a dam, irrigation ditch, schoolhouse, road and fences. The school began in 1876 school began. The Indian agent's sister-in-law taught reading, writing and arithmetic. The children loved to sing songs in class.

An old medicine man, named Oytes grew jealous of Agent Sam Parrish. He made the Paiute pay him money, so that he would not cast a spell on them. Oytes boasted that a white man's bullet would not kill him. The Agent grew tired of him. He offered to shoot Oytes for $300.00. The shaman fell to his knees and begged Parrish not to shoot him. The old man changed and began to do work and cooperate. Things had gone well for the Paiute people, up to that time. Then, Sam Parrish was transferred in 1876. A dishonest agent, named Rinehart, replaced him. He sold settlers Paiute lands and made them pay their own rations of food, blankets and clothing and gave the rest to his relatives.

When Chief Winnemucca and his Paiutes left Malheur Reservation, ytes led them to a supposed safe haven along the Malheur River. They were et there by a Bannock war-party, who was at war with the white eyes. 'innemucca and his band wanted no part of war. The shaman joined the rebels. eing at war, the Bannock war party took Chief Winnemucca II and the alheur Paiute people from the reservation captive, and stole their blankets, rses and weapons.

Sarah Winnemucca met with Captain Bernard and General Howard at 1eep's Camp. Determined to find her father, she rode to overtake the Bannock. om a high overlook Sarah surveyed the Bannock camp of several hundred epees. There were no sentries because of the high terrain. At nightfall Sarah scended the mountain slope, concealed under a blanket and war-paint and ole into her aging father's tent. She rescued him right out from under the annock's noses. During the night, she ushered her father out of the camp. Her other Lee, his wife, Mattie and cousin, John, who had come to help, held the rses and aided in the escape to Sheep Camp. From there, the army escorted rah, her father and family safely to Fort McDermott. Later, Sarah and Mattie ould work for General Howard as army scouts. The newspapers referred to her Princess Winnemucca. Sarah was made honorary chief of the Northern Paiute be for saving her people.

On January I, 1879 the Paiute Indians from Malheur Reservation began forced march to the Yakima reservation in southern Washington. They were rced to walk for hundreds of miles in sub zero temperatures. This trek became 1own as the "Paiute Trail of Tears." On the march, one hundred people died. 1e elderly and the young were most vulnerable to the cold and hunger. Thirty 1ys later they arrived to find that there was no food rations for them. Again, ere was starvation. The agent there was a Mr. Wilber. He would not help the 1iute people nor release them to go back home. Sarah begged him, but he came infuriated and threatened to jail her. The Paiute attempting to escape ere hunted down.

It was then that Sarah became a real champion for her people. She rote letters to Washington and toured and made speeches. On January 1, 1880 e government paid her expenses to travel all the way to Washington D.C. to e the, the Secretary of the Interior, who was over the Bureau of Indian Affairs, d President Rutherford B. Hayes. She told them about the half naked and arving Indians and the horrible conditions they had endured. Secretary Carl 1urtz signed a paper, saying that they could return to Malheur Reservation. 1ch family was to receive a plot of land. Any Paiutes working off of the servation could remain. Chief Winnemucca boarded the train for Nevada earing a brand new suit, a gift from the Bureau of Indian Affairs. Sarah carried order from Washington to restore the reservation. The words on paper were gus and their promises were all broken. Sarah felt betrayed.

Sarah later married Lambert Hopkins in Montana in 1882, but she ntinued to petition Washington. The wealthy Peabody sisters of Boston took her cause. One was a famous publisher. They funded lectures and aided her

cause. Army officers, judges and government officials lauded her. Her boo
"Life among the Paiutes," was published in 1883. It contained important lette
from the Indian Bureau and gained her support. She demanded that Congre
restore Malheur Reservation and remove the whites.

In July of 1884, Congress passed a law that granted land on t
Pyramid reservation would be given to Chief Winnemucca and the Paiute
Additional land was set aside for any Paiutes that had fled. Chief Winnemuc
who had died in 1882 did not see their triumph.

The Peabody sisters built a school for the Paiute children on Natchez
farm near Lovelock. Sarah taught 25 students for two years, until the scho
closed. She and her husband both died of tuberculosis four years apart, Sar
died October, 1891. Paiutes have carried on her legacy to fight for the people.

BIGFOOT

Starr Wilkinson was a 6 foot 8 inch, 300 pound half-breed, son of
Cherokee-negro mother and a white father. He began his trip west around 185
from St. Louis by wagon-train. He loved a girl, named Jesse Smith, who jilt
him for her new lover, Mr. Hart, who was an artist from New York. Wilkins
caught them lying in the sagebrush. He fought Hart and drowned him in t
Snake River. Young Wilkinson panicked and ran. On the run Wilkinson joined
Paiute Indian band who called him "Nampa," in Paiute, or "Bigfoot." He becan
their chief. The wagon-train returned to St. Louis, due to harsh winter. On the
return trip, "Nampa" and his Paiute band massacred all of the passenge
(including his ex-girlfriend) and burned the wagons. He led the renegades
stagecoach raids, along Reynolds Creek, on the Boise-Silver City road. On the
raids the man (who never rode a horse) ran alongside the moving stage coac
giving war-whoops, putting fear into the passengers. The outlaws robbed stag
near the mining town of Silver City.

Army investigators detected a bare seventeen and one half in
footprint along the Weiser River. The story of a mysterious giant appeared in t
Idaho Statesman Newspaper with an offer of a $1,000.00 reward, DEAD
ALIVE for "BIGFOOT." As Nampa ran alongside the stagecoach, Jo
Wheeler, a bounty hunter, was poised in the Aspen trees nearby with his
caliber long-rifle. Wheeler fired with his repeating rifle. Bigfoot disappear
from sight. Then Wheeler noticed a tumble-weed moving along the ground a
commenced firing. The hulk began running wildly toward him. Wheeler la
claimed that he shot Bigfoot 16 times total. Wheeler apologized for killing hi
Before he died, Bigfoot told Wheeler his life story, in exchange for giving him
customary Indian burial, in 1868. He was just 30 years old. Nampa.a became t
namesake of Nampa, Idaho. The "Bigfoot" legend didn't end there. Rumors a
that Bigfoot's ghost still roams the Owyhee desert.

In 1872, Smohalla, a Nez Perce prophet, proclaimed that Indians wou
rise up from the dead and drive the white-eyes out of the land. He initiated t
Dreamer's Religion Wavoca, a Paiute holy man in Nevada, whom the whit

called Jack Wilson, had a vision of immortal warriors in Ghost shirts dancing in a circle, invincible to white man's bullets. He started the "Ghost Shirt Religion."

The frenzy spread, influencing hundreds of Indians to rally and fight the white man with hope of redemption. Brule Sioux Chief Crow Dog was active in the Ghost Shirt Dance Movement. He is known for killing Brule Sioux Chief Spotted Tail. Word traveled fast about the Ghost Dance in Nevada to Fort Hall and on to the Plains, reaching the Sioux by 1890. Young Sioux braves did the Ghost Dance in their sacred shirts late in the night giving war-whoops, shooting rifles and dancing around a huge bonfire at Wounded Knee. It frightened nearby settlers, so the U.S. Cavalry was called in the next day. Chief Sitting Bull was pulled from his sleeping robes and shot. The Ghost Shirt religion caused the death of a famous Indian Medicine Man, Sitting Bull and hundreds of Sioux Indians at the Massacre of Wounded Knee by the U.S. Army. Sitting Bull's death was the passing of an era.

The largest reservations in Nevada are Duck Valley, Fort McDermott, Pyramid Lake, and Walker River. There are many smaller reservations and colonies, such as, Fallon Indian Reservation, Nevada, Fort Bidwell Indian Reservation, California, Summit Lake Paiute Tribe, Nevada, Warm Springs Indian Reservation, in Oregon. Indian Colonies are Bridgeport Paiute Indian Colony, California, Fallon Colony, Reno-Sparks Indian Colony and Winnemucca Colony in Nevada. Paiute Indians are now represented at Fort Hall Indian Reservation in eastern Idaho.

In 1952, nine hundred Paiute Indians lived at the Pyramid Lake Indian Reservation. The Bureau of Indian Affairs began a relocation program to place Indians in mainstream American life. Many that had left have returned, not liking the busy city life. They live on cattle and fish and they sell permits to fish and hunt on the reservation.

\# 29. Coeur d'Alene Chiefs and Wives-Salish Indians of the
Northwest (Courtesy of the Idaho State Historical Society)

Chapter Four
COEUR D' ALENE INDIANS

The Salish Indians came from a large stock of Salishan speakers in North America. They were referred to as the Salishan tribes and separated into three divisions: the Canadian Salish, Coastal Salish and Inland or Interior Salish in America. The Coastal Salish neighbored the Kwakiutl and Nootka Indians. They dwelled on the mainland coast.

They didn't make totem poles. They did display creativity by carving ceremonial masks, house-posts, mortuary posts and welcoming figures (some reaching 24 feet in height). Their women handcrafted gorgeous baskets in which they wove intricate designs. These Salish women were weavers of beautiful fringed blankets made from the wool of domestic long-haired dogs and mountain goats. With the coming of the Hudson's Bay Company trading posts the Salish people were able to obtain beautiful fine quality multicolored Hudson's Bay blankets

The Coastal Salish carved magnificent ocean-going sturgeon-nosed dug-out canoes. Coastal Salish Indian's main food staple was fish; their diet included deer and wild goat. Potlatch was a ceremonial practice by the Coastal tribes in which lavish gifts were given by the host to guests, often kinsmen. Sometimes material gifts were destroyed to display the host's wealth.

Long before the coming of the white man coastal Indians devised a monetary system called wampum. A mussel shell was initially broken into pieces by a stone hammer. Each piece was then rounded by abrasion. A hole was drilled in the center with a bow-drill. The shell discs were put on a leather thong to be worn around the neck. Wampum was exchanged in trade. The Indians established a value for a bead strand early on. They called the strands bead money.

Prehistoric Salish Indians lived in the San Juan Islands. Archeologists discovered shell middens on the islands and artifacts. Middens are mounds of clamshells piled on one another in elevated layers, showing years of habitation. A Clovis style projectile point was discovered in that region dating back to 11,500 B.P.

THE INTERIOR SALISH

The Coeur d'Alene Indians called themselves the Schee-chu'umsh or the Skitswish people, which was translated, "Discovered People" or "Those who are found here." The Coeur d'Alene people, as well as the Kalispel Indians speak the Salish language. French fur traders gave them a nickname, "Coeur d'Alene Indians," meaning "heart of the awl" or "pointed hearts," in French. The French, who traded with them proclaimed them to be the finest traders in the world.

The Coeur d'Alene people shared a common language and maintained a close relationship with their Upper Salish counterparts who are now in Montana, present day Washington, Canada and with the coastal Salish on the Pacific coast.

Theirs was a strong alliance with the Interior Salish. Fishing resources were shared, as well as trade fairs and gala celebrations. They were neighboring tribes and allies in war. In prehistoric times Coeur d'Alene Indian males married captured women. After the horse, intermarriage occurred peacefully between the various tribes.

Coeur d'Alene Indian country began west of the Bitterroot and Coeur d'Alene Mountains to the headwaters of the Spokane River and extended above Spokane Falls to Coeur d'Alene Lake and all of the tributaries leading into the lake. Their boundaries to the southwest extended across the Clearwater River and to the west taking in De Smet and Hangman Creek, included the south side of the Spokane River and Spokane Valley.

The Coeur d'Alene Indians dwelled in the vicinity of Lake Coeur d'Alene and the St. Joe River for centuries. Four major bands existed. They were the Spokane River, Spokane Valley, Coeur d'Alene River and the St. Joe River bands. They fished in the Coeur d'Alene River. Indigenous fish caught in the Coeur d'Alene River were Chinook salmon, mountain whitefish, rainbow trout and the west slope cutthroat trout.

A stone weir was a kind of dam used in the river to capture wild native fish. The dam trapped and slowed the fish. They used baskets, bone hooks, gaff hooks, harpoons, hook and line, nets, spears and traps to catch the fish. Salish fishing grounds were shared, as were trade fairs and celebrations that brought the Coeur d'Alene Indians and other Salish from all around.

The fishing villages were formed from extended family groups. These groups came together to form one large composite band and were socio-politically allied to other Interior Salish, as well as neighboring tribes. The Coeur d'Alene lived in permanent fishing villages on Lake Coeur d'Alene and on the Coeur d'Alene River. The Coeur d'Alene people were fishermen like the Kalispel. Coeur d'Alene Lake was the site of their main village. Wild fish caught in the 31,400 acre Coeur d'Alene Lake by the Salish Indians were bull trout, Chinook salmon, kokanee salmon, mountain whitefish, rainbow trout and west slope cutthroat trout.

West of the Coeur d'Alene Indians were the Spokane people. The Kalispel and Pend d' Oreille were on their northern border. On their east side dwelled the Flathead Indians in the Bitterroot Valley. The Nez Perce Indians were on their southern border. Neutral ground divided the two tribes to keep the peace. Nez Perce, Palouse and Spokane Indians shared the camas fields in the southwest. This was in Palouse country.

The Coeur d'Alene had a combined council of male and female members. The council chose the chief, who sometimes came from the same family. These Indians had a band chief or headman. He might have had assistants. His role was similar to the headman of the Shoshoni. It was a permanent position. The band chief could have been chosen as war-leader. The war leader was to have been a strong warrior. His duties were to act as war-chief on the hunt or in battle.

These Salish Indians practiced polygamy like the Shoshoni Indians. Sororate polygyny was also practiced by the husband, taking brides of his wife's sisters. This was usually the case if a man had any wealth. In the reverse a bride would marry brothers. If the wife died, the sororate rule applied. The husband married her oldest sister. If the husband passed, his brother married the brother's widow and her sisters. This mode is called levirate polygamy. Divorce in the tribe was rare. The Coeur d'Alene's were sturdy built. Men were stout, muscular. They averaged around 5' 8" tall. Women averaged about 5' 6" in height and were generally slim, with attractive features.

The Coeur d'Alene practiced child betrothal. An agreement was reached between both their parents. The children then were subject to rearranged marriage. Courtship of young maidens often included a chaperone. Sometimes young suitors would delve into magic involving love affairs. Love might be accomplished by seeking a vision, fasting or sweat baths. The marriage proposal was dramatized. At first, the suitor stood in the center of the lodge. Then, he sat and asked her questions. He told her that he loved her and would like to marry her. She would turn her face away from him and would not answer. He would then start a small handful of straw on fire on the ground. She would step back and put out the fire. Then, he would squeeze her foot or gently step down on it. If her response was, "Why do you step on my foot?" It was a sign and he went to ask permission of her parents. If their answer was yes, the wedding was on. The groom's parents arranged the wedding.

There was a gift exchange after the marriage. The newly-weds customarily moved in with the husbands' parents in the beginning like an engagement. The bride was not recognized until after the birth of their first child. It was important that the bride live in accord with the groom's parents. The Coeur d'Alene practiced a cross-cousin relationship. Aunts were as mothers and cousins were as siblings. A death was announced to the people by a town crier. The announcement was followed by intense wailing and the body remained in the lodge for two days. It was attended day and night by relatives or friends. The body was bathed, hair combed and the face was painted. The body was flexed and the arms were positioned so that the hands were clenched over the chest. It was bound in a deerskin, mummy-like and wrapped in a rabbit skin robe. A pole was used by the pall bearers to lift the body to the shoulders. It was carried to the grave and buried on a rocky slope. The shaman acted as overseer of speeches and eulogies. A ritual was performed by the shaman to rid the body of evil spirits. The lodge of the deceased was burned. The rest of the property was given as gifts to guests. The funeral was followed by a huge feast. The spouse of the deceased was in mourning for one year.

#30. Mission of the Sacred Heart of the Coeur d' Alene Indians
"Cataldo Mission" Oldest structure in Idaho

#31. Salish Village In the Pacific Northwest
(Courtesy of the Idaho State Historical Society)

MYTHOLOGY

The Coeur d'Alene, Palouse and the Spokane Indians tell the mythological tale of how Coyote created the Indian tribes. At the end of the mythical age of animals, Coyote, the old trickster, said that people would come. Long ago in Lake Cle Elum was a huge beaver monster, named Wishpoosh. He had fiery red eyes and giant claws. Wishpoosh would drown or eat the animal people that came to the lake. The animal people cried out to Coyote to save them from the giant beaver monster.

Not knowing what to do, Coyote asked his three sisters, who were huckleberries in his stomach. They refused to tell him. So, Coyote threatened to call hail down from the sky. They told him to make a huge spear and tie a line from it to his wrist. Coyote went to the lake and threw the spear into the monster's side. Wishpoosh roared in pain and dived deep into the lake, pulling Coyote down. On the bottom, they fought so hard that it shook the mountains around the lake, causing a huge hole. The water from the lake rushed through the hole and down the mountainside, creating a larger lake in the Kittias Valley.

Wishpoosh continued to roar and tried to drown Coyote, but Coyote hung on. The monster plunged eastward across the valley, digging the Yakima River. The waters overflowed and they dug a big lake in Walla-Walla country. Then the monster turned sharply to the west and cut out the channel of the Big River (Columbia River). Coyote held on to rocks and trees, tearing them loose making little waterfalls. Coyote hung on as the monster tore through the mountains, making the gorge of the Big River. Coyote almost drowned; muskrat laughed. Coyote decided to be rid of the beaver monster. He asked his three sisters, in the form of huckleberries in his stomach. After hearing their answer, he said, Yes I knew that all of the time. He turned himself into a fir tree branch, as the sister said, and floated out to the beaver monster. The monster swallowed him up, as his sisters predicted.

He changed himself back into his animal shape. Coyote took out his knife and hacked away at Wishpoosh's heart and killed the monster. Coyote made himself small and climbed out of the monster's throat. Muskrat helped Coyote pull the beaver monster onto the shore of the Big River.

Coyote again took out his sharp knife and carved the monster into pieces. From your body, Wishpoosh I will make a new race of people. From his loins, Coyote made the Chinook Indians to live and trade at the mouth of the Big River (Columbia River). Others shall face the big ocean and spear salmon and dig clams. You shall be short, fat and have weak legs. From the monster's legs, he made the Klickitat Indians. You will dwell along the rivers flowing from the big white mountain, north of Big River. You will be of good wit, fast runners and great horsemen.

From the monster's arms, Coyote made the Cayuse Indians. You 'will be powerful with the bow and arrows and war clubs. From the ribs, Coyote made the Yakima Indians. You will live on the Yakima River, east of the mountains. You will help and protect the poor. From the head, Coyote created *the Nez Perce Indians. You shall live in the valley of the Kooskia and the Walla-Walla Rivers. You will be men of brains, and good at making speeches. You will be skilled horsemen and brave warriors.*

Coyote took the remains and created the Snake River Indians. You shall be people of violence. You will hunt the buffalo and travel far and wide. And so it was that Coyote created the tribes from pieces of the beaver monster. He went back up the Big River. Coyote forgot to make mouths for the Coastal people and to open their eyes. He found hungry people wandering around with their eyes closed. Coyote took his now dull knife and cut slits for their eyes and mouth. They now have ugly mouths.

THE HORSE

The acquisition of the horse, by the prehistoric Coeur d'Alene Indians soon led to buffalo hunts on the Great Plains. The hunt leader was chosen as a war leader, since the fierce Blackfoot and Crow tribes would be encountered on the hunt. The Coeur d'Alene joined with neighboring tribes to further expand their numbers and for military strength on their hunting excursions. The Colville, Kutenai, Nez Perce, Upper and Lower Pend d' Oreille, Spokane and Shoshoni were allies who the Coeur d'Alene joined on the hunt. In the late 1700's, millions of buffalo roamed the Great Plains. It took dozens of buffalo to feed a whole band of Indians over the long winter. Buffalo meat and robes were hauled on pack horses on the long trip home from the Great Plains. Hunting on the Plains for years, the Coeur d'Alene began to imitate the Plains Indians. They adopted the idea of chiefs and sub-chiefs and a military hierarchy. A war leader led sub-chiefs in battle. Headdresses, deerskin clothing, and teepees were adopted. They began smoking the "peace pipe" with their allies, a Plains Indian tradition.

The Interior Salish dwelled east of British Columbia, bordering the Kootenai Tribe. The Coeur d' Alene Indians lodged in the land that became eastern Washington State, along the Spokane Basin. They fished on the Columbia River in the Bitterroot Mountains in western Montana Territory and lakes in northern Idaho Territory. The Salish Indians, like the Algonquin Nation, in Northern America, made up a large nation covering a vast range. The Coeur d'Alene tribe was divided into three bands and dwelled along the Coeur d'Alene and St. Joe Rivers in what is now called Palouse Country in present day northern Idaho for thousands of years. They dwelled on Hayden and Pend Oreille lakes in massive sedentary villages. Their territory extended over five million acres.

The Palouse country was a favorite haunt of the Coeur d'Alene Indians. Steptoe Butte towered into the heavens, one thousand feet above the landscape. The solid stone grassy butte was a shrine used for centuries by the Salish for meditation, prayer and sacred ceremonies for centuries.

Indian girls reaching womanhood when they began to menstruate were banned to the menstrual hut. They purified themselves first by bathing, and then meditated in the hut, on becoming women.

Pregnant young Salish women, close to delivery went into special birthing huts before the baby was born like the Shoshoni Indians and most American Indian tribes. Midwives assisted in childbirth and due to difficulties, a shaman might have assisted, but the husband was never asked to help. It was believed that screaming in pain during labor would cause misfortune. Rituals were performed over the infant to make sure it was healthy and to become successful. The baby's head was gently shaped. The Infant was bathed in a birch bark container. Ten days after delivery, the young mother returned to her regular activities besides caring for the baby. Parents and friends gave gifts to the mother and child by the parents and friends.

One present always given was a cradleboard. The cradleboard was constructed from a long oval board. The upper section was wrapped with cloth or deerskin to hold the infant. The upper cradle was beaded with bright beads and decorated by geometric animal figures. Straps went over the mother's shoulders to hold the cradleboard on her back. The infant was carried in a cradleboard on the mothers back for almost two years, before the child would learn to walk.

At this time another type of child carrier, made of deerskin, was carried like a sling over the mother's neck. This apparatus allowed the youngster's arms and legs to protrude.

Boys and girls were sent out on receive their vision quests around age twelve. The vision quest was normally accompanied by fasting, bathing, meditation and religious purification to cleanse them of evil spirits. Sweat lodges were used at a fairly young age. An animal spirit was usually contacted in a vision. An animal, usually an eagle or bear was the norm. This animal became their spirit guide for life.

The Coeur d'Alene, like the Kutenai, used the horse and traveled onto the Plains to hunt buffalo. They had political allies with them on the hunt. The Coeur d'Alene Indians felt safer in numbers and were accompanied by the Flatheads, Nez Perce, Pend d' Oreille, and Spokane Indians on their expedition to the Plains.

Sometimes the hunting party became more militant with a war-chief. The camp was laid out in a circle for protection from possible enemies. The posture of the hunt was often more a military one than a hunting organization. Scouts on horseback formed a large circle. When they located the herd, a signal was given to the other Indians. A prize bison was selected and the hunt was on.

#32. Defiant Coeur **d'Alene** Chieftains-
(Courtesy of the Idaho State Historical Society

The "Heart of the Awl" people dwelt in a huge permanent village along e Spokane and St. Joe Rivers, Lake Coeur d'Alene and Lake Hayden and the ꓲlouse country. They lived on about five million acres.

LEWIS AND CLARK

On May 6, 1806, Lewis and Clark were first to make contact with the ꓳeur d'Alene Indians and record it. He described the Clearwater River and ꓵke Coeur d'Alene in his writings. The Indians met Lewis and Clark along the ꓲearwater River. On their return trip from the Oregon Coast, Clark wrote about e Coeur d'Alene and Spokane Indian mat huts. One native gave Clark a whide whip. Some of Lewis and Clark's writing about them was nearly ꓲentical.

Lewis met three Skeet-so-mish Natives that resided at the falls of a rge river, which emptied into the Columbia River. Lewis made a remark that ꓰy look and dress like the Chopenish Indians, but their language was radically fferent and he could not understand their vocabulary.

Clark met a Nez Perce warrior whose nose had been severed by a ꓲake Indian warrior's lance. His name was Cut Nose. Clark administered ꓰdical attention to the Nez Perce and described a huge native dwelling for ꓩht families; he said was like an ancient apartment dwelling.

When David Thompson of the Northwest Company arrived among the ꓳeur d'Alene in 1809, they gave him a gift of fish, dried salmon, berries and ꓲtelope meat. At that time there were 80 men and their families.

Thompson told the Coeur d'Alene Indians that they were going to have quit gambling and go out and trap some beaver and other mammals if they ꓮnted something to have to trade for guns, ammunition and steel arrowheads. ꓰey did not want him to build a trading post and were not friendly. The fur ꓲder lived among the Indians and learned their language. In addition to trading ꓲth them he married Indian women and raised their children.

Since prehistoric times, the Coeur d'Alene maintained a trade route ꓳm the Great Plains to the Pacific Ocean. The Interior Salish Indians made nual trips to the Pacific to meet with their Coastal Salish trade partners to rter.

The Coeur d'Alene Indians heard from other tribes about the Jesuit ack Robes and their medicine men. They asked the priest to come and live ꓲong them, because of the influence of the Jesuit priests.

Father Pierre Jean De Smet, the Sacred Heart Mission was established the St. Joe River in 1841. The Jesuits Christianized the Coeur d'Alene Indians er the next decade. Father Nicholas Point built the Sacred Heart Mission using ꓰgy, laymen and the local Indians to construct a magnificent cathedral. The ꓲsion was later renamed, De Smet Mission.

In 1848, the mission was relocated to a site near the Coeur d'Alene ver, due to severe flooding. In 1853, the mission included a parish, farm and ꓰlve log cabin quarters for the Indians and covered around 3,000 acres. The

livestock there included horses, mules, oxen, pigs and milk cows and becam
known as the Church of the Sacred Heart or Cataldo Mission. Jesuit Prie
Nicholas Point kept a journal. He recorded his meetings with the various Indi
tribes in his oil paintings.

There is a smaller Church of the Sacred Heart is in De Smet, Idah
Cataldo Mission is the oldest standing building in Idaho. The Cataldo Mission
on Old Mission State Park land and recently faced closure, but the Coe
d'Alene tribe has fought it. There is a 25 year agreement with the Parks syste
allowing the mission to remain in its present location. It remains there, today.

INDIAN WAR IN THE PLATEAU REGION

The Indian Wars in the Plateau region commenced with the Cayu
War of 1847. The Cayuse Indians lost half of their tribe to measles from conta
with the Whitman mission. In 1847 they massacred Marcus and Narcis
Whitman and nine others.

Cornelius Gilliam led 500 white settlers in attacks on the Plate
Indians, in retaliation for the Whitman Massacre. From 1848-49 the Cayu
Indians hid in the Blue Mountains, but in the autumn of 1849, they handed ov
five Indian fugitives that had participated in the Whitman massacre. Arreste
were Kimasumpkin, Klokamas, Isaiachalkis, Tiloukaikt and Tomahas. All fi
were convicted and hanged in 1850.

Treaties were signed in 1854, west of the Cascades; the governor h
hoped to have put the Indians on reservations and on June 1855, held the Wal
Walla Council. Three treaties were signed for the natives in the northeaste
Plateau. In the first Treaty, the Cayuse, Umatilla and Walla-Walla tribal lan
were reduced from four million acres to 95,000 acres. In the second Trea
fourteen tribal groupings agreed to go onto the Yakima Reservation. The thi
Treaty confined the Nez Perce to their reservation in parts of Washingto
Oregon and west-central Idaho Territories.

In July of 1855, the Flathead Council produced the Flathead Treaty a
ceded Flathead, Kutenai and Upper Pend d' Oreille lands In Idaho and Monta
to the United States. Three tribes were placed on the Montana Territo
reservation.

On September 23, 1855, Indian Agent Andrew Bolon was killed I
Chief Kamiakin's nephew, Moshell and two other Yakima warriors. In respon
to the murder, Major Haller and U.S. troops attacked Chief Kamiakin and t
Yakima's in the Battle of Toppenish. On November 9, 1855, at Union Ga
Major Gabriel Rains led the Regulars and Volunteers against the Yakin
Indians, forcing them to retreat. Rains continued on, he obliterated Sainte Cro
Mission and the camp of Chief Kamiakin, at Ahtanum Creek, along with oth
missions in Yakima territory.

The Blackfoot Council on October 16, 1855 was conducted at t
mouth of the Judith River by Governor Stevens. A peace treaty was written a
signed by the Blackfoot, Flathead, Kutenai, Nez Perce, and Pend d' Orei

tribes. The treaty created shared buffalo hunting in Blackfoot territory, east of the Rockies.

Settlers' cattle grazed on Indian grasses and there was unrest with the Indians, east of the Cascade Mountains at this time. The Indians felt gratified to steal the settlers' cows. Gold was discovered on the Yakima Reservation in 1855.

The same year, miners swarmed onto the Yakima Reserve causing more conflict. The Yakima War followed, led by Chief Kamiakin. The Yakima's incited neighboring tribes to rebel. The Cayuse and Walla-Walla Indians soon joined them. The Yakima Indian War was fought from 1855-1856. In 1856, three military forts were built in Yakima country along the Columbia River. They were Basket Fort, Fort Simcoe and Fort Walla-Walla. This angered the Yakima, more. July 10, 1856, Benjamin Shaw and Volunteers massacred a peaceful Cayuse Camp in the Grand Ronde Valley. Stevens held Council with the Indians. Later, Stevens' party was attacked by warriors, and repelled by Colonel Steptoe's troops. Walla-Walla Valley was closed to settlers.

THE COEUR d' ALENE WAR

In 1858, there was an outcry to the military by white settlers in Colville, for protection from the local Indians. The Indians were becoming upset with the settlers. Their young braves spoke of war, which broke out with the local Indians.

On May 4, 1858, Colonel Edward Steptoe led 155 soldiers, with Nez Perce guides to Fort Colville, to check out the settler's claims against the Indians. Colonel Steptoe suffered defeat by a large group of Coeur d'Alene, Palouse and Spokane Indians, in the Battle of Tohotonimme (later called the Battle of Steptoe). The Coeur d'Alene War (also called the Spokane War) began in 1858. It involved the Coeur d'Alene, Northern Paiute, Palouse, Spokane and Yakima Indians.

In August of 1858, Colonel George Wright led an expedition of 600 troops against the Coeur d'Alene, Palouse and Spokane Indians who had conquered Steptoe's forces. The Indians faced defeat, September 1 1858, at the battle of Four Lakes and again at the Battle of Spokane Plain, on September 5, 1858. On the ninth of September, Wright's forces captured 900 horses. They spent two days killing 700 horses in order to limit the Indians' movement. The camp was called "Horse Slaughter Camp."

#33. Coeur d'Alene Indian Princesses on Horseback-
(Courtesy of the Idaho State Historical society)

On September 17, 1858, Colonel Wright held council with the Coeur d'Alene Indians at the Coeur d'Alene Mission to dictate the terms of surrender in the "Treaty of Peace and Friendship."

Five days later, the Spokane accepted terms of surrender on Latah Creek, with nearly the same terms. The ex surrendered to Wright on the Palouse River. September 24, 1858, Colonel Wright hanged Yakima Chief Qualchan for war crimes. Wright also hanged Palouse Indians for deaths of soldiers during the Steptoe Campaign.

On October 1, 1866, the Coeur d'Alene reservation in northern Idaho was recognized by Executive Order of President Grant. In 1869, U.S. President Grant created the Board of Indian Commissioners. He initiated a peace policy to end Indian Wars in the west and reform of the Indian Service.

Silver was discovered in the Idaho panhandle in 1870, which created a rush of mining activity.

In 1871 the U.S. Congress ended the process of making treaties with Indians. They sponsored programs for wholesale slaughter of the buffalo in order to force the Indians onto reservations (1871-1879).

#34. Coeur d'Alene Indian Chieftain Horsemen
(Courtesy of the Idaho State Historical Society)

RESERVATIONS

Their range had been 4 million acres, but treaties reduced their reserve its present size. The sale of their lands in 1889 amounted to only three dollars acre for some of the richest farming, timber and mining land available. The nited States still honors the purchase. The Coeur d'Alene Indian Reservation as originally 590,000 acres.

In 1887, the Coeur d'Alene people moved onto their reservation in aho. The Coeur d'Alene made the transition from hunters and gatherers, to riculture in a short period of time. An industrious people, they soon had oductive farms, good houses, barns, gardens, horses, cattle, hogs, ducks, ickens, wagons and farm implements

The Coeur d'Alene Reservation originally included all of Lake Coeur Alene and has been reduced to half of Lake Coeur d'Alene and a segment of louse Country. According to the Homestead Act of 1906, the reservation was duced to 58,000 acres.

The Coeur d'Alene Indian Reservation was established in 1873 and is cated in Benewah County, Idaho, south of the city of Coeur d'Alene, Idaho (in e panhandle). The reservation is on the western edge of the Rockies. Steptoe utte is a sacred Coeur d'Alene shrine. Towns within the Coeur d'Alene Indian eservation are presently, De Smet, Plummer, Tensed and Worley, Idaho. Coeur Alene Indians sponsor a powwow annually at Worley.

#35. Kalispel Indian Maiden from the Idaho Plateau is beautifully bedecked in *seashells, earrings and necklace. Her braided hair has otter fur and weasel skin dangles.
(Courtesy of AZUSA PUBLISHING, LLC

#36. Coastal Salish Native of the Northwest Coast (Courtesy of AZUSA PUBLISHING, LLC)

Chapter Five
KALISPEL INDIANS (PEND D' OREILLE)

The Kalispel Indians speak the Salish language. The way the Kalispel spell Salish is Selis (pronounced Sehlish). Salish is a large linguistic family in the Pacific Northwest.

The Coastal Kalispel tribe lived off the ocean essentially. Inland Kalispel Indians fished from canoes on the Columbia River. Archeological digs there reveal early man, existing 11,500 years B.P.

The Kalispel Indian tribe was widespread, ranging from southern Canada (British Columbia) and from the inland Northwest (now Washington State) along the Columbia River eastward into Montana (the Upper Kalispel) and Idaho.

The Western Kalispel Indian did intermarry with Colville, Chewela, and Spokane Indians. The tribe ranged, from British Columbia along the Pend Oreille River in E. Washington and Idaho, around Lake Pend Oreille, Priest Lake, on the lower Clark Fork River and the Montana "Horse Plains."

An ancient Kalispel Indian trade route that extended from the Spokane River through Rathdrum Prairie and crossed the Pend Oreille River at the "Sineacateen," (Kalispel for river crossing), near Laclede, and crossed the Kootenai River at Bonner's Ferry. Lewis and Clark arrived in Kalispel Country, 1805.

The Montana Kalispel dwelled and fished along the Kalispel River drainage, also hunted and foraged for food. The Horse Plains divided the Upper from the Lower Kalispel.

They hunted buffalo on the Montana Plain. Buffalo jumps were used by the Pend d' Oreille Indians to run buffalo over a cliff. If this did not kill the bison, a v-shaped corral below was used to ensnare them. Another type of hunting buffalo was the decoy method.

The v-shaped trap was employed again on a steep incline. One hunter would don a buffalo robe, complete with horns and would get down on all fours and crawl in among the herd and bleat like a baby buffalo. Buffalo have a keen sense of smell, but very poor eyesight.

As the decoy crawled away from the herd, the dumb buffalo followed him into the corral. The decoy then squeezed out through an opening that the buffalo could not.

The band of hunters moved in and slaughtered the beast with bow and arrows. Buffalo were butchered, the meat jerked.

The Kalispel got the horse in the 1700's and could ride to the Upper Missouri to hunt the buffalo. They joined the buffalo-horse culture. Blackfoot raiders often stole Kalispel horses. The horse brought the teepee and the Plains life-way.

"CAMAS PEOPLE"

Lower Kalispel Indians dwelled mainly around Lake Pend Oreille, along the Pend Oreille River, on Priest Lake and Lake Kalispel in what is now Idaho. They were a tribe of hunters, diggers, and fishermen. They hunted and fished, while the women gathered. The Pend d' Oreille Indian men were passive, but would fight if necessary.

The women, like the Snake Indians, were diggers. They foraged for roots and gathered berries, nuts, seeds and other edible plants. Women made fine baskets of cedar and mat. They cared for their family and cooked meals.

The Pend d' Oreille was Salish peoples who depended on the fishing industry in prehistoric times. Other Salish peoples were normally always allies. They fished the Palouse River in eastern Washington and the northern Idaho panhandle. They shared fishing territory with the Colville, Flathead and Spokane Indians. The Pend d' Oreille Indians fished from the Columbia River to Flathead Lake in their bark covered canoes. Fish made up a major portion of their diet.

The Kalispel in what is now Idaho dwelled mostly around Lake Kalispel and were called "Lake Kalispel Indians," by the white man. It was rich in land-locked Kokanee Salmon, rainbow trout and whitefish. They also lived on Lake Pend d' Oreille. If they lived on the Pend d' Oreille River or Lake Pend d' Oreille, they were called Pend d' Oreille Indians. Kalispel or Pend d' Oreille Indians are two names for the same Salish tribe. These tribes were named for the locality where they lived.

In other regions they utilized rock weirs to create dams to capture fish. The Coeur d'Alene Indians were their neighbors to the northwest. The Pend d' Oreille Indians lived in close proximity to the Flathead Indians and intermarried with them and the Coeur d'Alene, Nez Perce and Spokane. Kalispel, Flathead, Kutenai, and other Salish bands, who shared Lake Pend Oreille, dwelled and fished there. The Pend d' Oreille Indians were nomadic and moved in rhythmic cycles to gather food.

Kalispel in their native tongue means "Camas People." French fur trappers came in contact with the Kalispel Indians and gave them a nickname, calling them," Pend d' Oreille Indians," meaning ear pendant, since they practiced piercing their ears for adornment. They wore large shell earrings, traded from their Coastal Salish counterparts. They adorned themselves with beads, hair adornment, pierced earrings and tattoos. Often, they were called Flathead Indians, also Salish Indians, mistaking them for the Salish Coastal Indians.

The Kalispel Indians spent their summers on Lake Pend' Oreille fishing, gathering berries and other foods. There were many camas fields along the Pend d' Oreille River. In autumn they dug camas and hunted buffalo. In the winter they moved to Montana territory. The "Camas people" dug the camas root annually, in the autumn.

A six foot square fire pit was dug and filled with a layer of smooth stones. A fire was built on top of the stones. Red hot stones were covered with a layer of grass and camas roots were laid on top. This was covered with earth and a fire built over it. The fire was kept burning for 24 hours. The tubers were placed in willow baskets to cool. The camas was made into bread, cake or porridge. The excess was stored underground, for winter or ground in a mortar and pestle, into meal. The meal was baked into camas bread. Surplus camas was traded.

The Kalispel Indians migrated in the spring to Spokane country to dig couse (bitter root and wild onion). The tubers were cured in the sun. Wild onion was mixed with black moss and baked under red hot stones

Chokecherries and service berries were picked and stored for winter. The berries were ground in a mortar and pestle into a pudding texture. These were mixed with strips of buffalo meat and fat, ground and pressed into cakes, called pemmican. Salmon were caught and dried in shade to slow the drying process.

Kalispel Indians dwelt on Lake Kalispel and depended on fish. The Lake Kalispel Indians intermarried with Nez Perce Indians and several Salish speaking tribes. One tribe would act as bride-donor for the other. Many members of the tribe had mixed lineage. Regardless, they still maintained their identity.

The Pend' Oreille dwelled in teepees in the summer and "tule huts" in the winter. Tule huts were a framework fastened to a tree limb for support, covered with woven tule mats, made from cattails. Cattails grew there in abundance along creeks and marshes. They ate the cattail bulb, the size of a potato.

THE PEND D'OREILLE GREET LEWIS & CLARK

In 1805, Lewis and Clark arrived in Kalispel Indian Territory. On September 4, 1805, a village numbering four hundred Pend d' Oreille Indians was encamped in the Bitterroot Valley, in what would become western Montana. Smoke curled upwards from campfires in front of many teepees. Their warriors readied themselves for the tiring trek to hunt the buffalo. Women were busy picking choke-cherries. Horses grazed on cool grasses, as children played and dogs barked.

A curious group of ragtag adventurers approached their camp in peace. It was the Lewis and Clark Expedition. They were on route to the Pacific Ocean. The Pend d' Oreille was friendly and offered to help them. Pend d' Oreille Indians chuckle as they recall a story of Lewis and Clark, in 1805.

Seeing the pale faces of the party, the chiefs ordered fur blankets laid on the ground for them to sit on, fearing that they were cold. The traveling party called them the "Coospeller." Soon after meeting this party, they met the Hudson's Bay Company traders. The Kalispel Indians occupied the Bitterroot Valley until 1800. They were forced out, when French traders supplied guns and ammunition to their foes, the Algonquin Indians. Flathead Indians then occupied the valley. The Bitterroot people intermarried with the Nez Perce.

Indian Meadow once was a grassy plain, a perfect site for Indian ponies to graze. Its Pend d' Oreille name was Nacemi. It served the Pend d' Oreille tribe as a ceremonial ground, in the summer and autumn.

There was an ancient Kalispel Indian trade route that extended from the Spokane River and Rathdrum Prairie and crossed the Pend Oreille River at the Sineacateen, meaning river crossing, in the Kalispel dialect, near the present day, Laclede. The trail continued northward across the Kootenai River at Bonner's Ferry.

THE FUR TRADE

In 1809 the American Fur Trade Company established the Salish House among the Kalispel Indians. In 1810, David Thompson opened a fur trade post for the North West Company on Lake Pend d' Oreille. Thompson's trappers followed the Kalispel trail and built the Spokane House west of Spokane Falls. The city of Spokane was later established near there. Kalispel Indians did not hunt, but preferred to gamble and did not contribute to the post. Thompson's Kullyspell House was erected in a bad location, closing in 1811.

In 1823 Hudson's Bay trapper, Alexander Ross erected "Flathead Post," called the Second Salish House or "Kullyspell House," near Sand Point five miles east of Thompson Falls, in Flathead Indian country.

Ross's beaver brigade of 140 men, including Iroquois Indians, penetrated Idaho's Salmon River country reaping over 5,000 beaver skins that year, nearly depleting the beaver there. Peter Skene Ogden was beaver brigade leader in the Snake River basin, 1824¬1831 for the Hudson's Bay Company. James W. Dease and John Work were added in the field drainage. Brigade leader, John Work, traded from Fort Nez Perce and was a fair Hudson's Bay trader with the Blackfoot and Salish in the field. Axes, beads, blankets, coffee, coffee, guns, knives, mirrors, pipes and tobacco were exchanged for Furs.

THE BLACK ROBES

In 1841, French Jesuit missionaries, Father De Smet, Nicholas Point and a Dutch priest, Adrian Hoecking came to Christianize and baptize the Blackfoot, Coeur d'Alene, Flathead and Kalispel Indians. They lived in brush huts, like the Indians.

Father De Smet spent six years among the Interior Indians, having crossed the ocean many times. The Coeur d'Alene's asked Father De Smet to build a mission school on their land. Protestant missionaries also came and built missions among them. Some converted to Christianity. The Kalispel received the Jesuit Catholic "Black robes (Kaniksu, in the Kalispel tongue) and their religion. Father Pierre Jean De Smet and the Jesuits were a strong Christian influence on the Kalispel Indians. De Smet Christianized Kalispel Chief "Standing Grizzly," baptizing him, Loyola. After that, He was a sort of "holy man." and brave leader and good hunter. He was loved by his people as a kind of

ther figure and recognized as an elder. The chief was also voted hunt leader
r the buffalo hunt. Chief Loyola died on April 6, 1846 and was succeeded by
ctor Alamiken, by election. Loyola had been a major witness and most
alispel accepted Catholicism. Others returned to their own ways. The native
ligion had been in force hundreds of years. Not all Kalispel were ready to
smiss their old beliefs. The Catholic Church dominated the Kalispel.

In 1845 wagons arriving in Oregon Territory came in a rhythm, at such
rate as to double the number of emigrants there. At the same time those wagon
ins brought smallpox to the Indians. The winter of 1846-47 killed hundreds of
g game animals in the region, because of heavy snows and cold.

The priests at the mission prayed that the animal population would
turn, but their prayers fell short. The clergy wanted the Indians to be God
aring farmers, so they built a village with a church, priest's house, stable, barn,
ops and a grist mill. There was flooding in 1845 and 1846, which ruined their
ops. A 160 acre plot was planted to grow potatoes and wheat at the St. Ignatius
ission, but the Indians were not too excited to trade hunting, fishing and root
gging for farming. Two severe winters followed.

A Blackfoot Indian raid on Saint Mary's, in 1850 caused such fear in
e community that the clergy in charge shut the mission down. The Kalispel
ded horses and canoes to Major John Owen, the trader who had purchased the
d St. Mary's mission. St. Ignatius was having problems, also. The Indians
came disillusioned in farming and returned to hunting, fishing and digging
ots to live. They traded for guns, cloth and continued hunting, warring and
ealing horses.

Miners and farmers overran Pend d' Oreille Indians lands. Traders sold
cohol to the Indians. The small pox killed roughly one third of the Northwest
dians.

The St. Ignatius was moved back to its old location on the Pend Oreille
ver in 1855 and Victor and his band returned to St. Ignatius journeying to
ontana Territory. The Pend d' Oreilles were lucky, however. They had been
ccinated for smallpox at the mission. Another band of St. Ignatius moved to
old location on the Pend Oreille River in 1855.

Victor and his band returned to St. Ignatius and journeyed, to Montana
rritory. Mission funds were depleted. Crops had failed and the game animals
led. In 1853 the Pend d' Oreille suffered from near starvation.

Gold was discovered in Colville Valley in 1854 at the mouth of the
nd' Oreille River. Gold rush fever struck the prospectors, who ran over
alispel Indian land by the thousands, like the Nez Perce had experienced. The
dians reacted by leaving for a buffalo hunt. Stevens called a council meeting at
. Ignatius. They did not show up for the council. Stevens wanted to sell their
ds and displace to the reserve, however they lacked a means of negotiation
ncerning land allocation.

The Kalispel Indians at St. Ignatius Mission on the Pend Oreille River
re in danger of losing their identity, as well as their autonomy by remaining

there. The Indians became hungry. By depending on the Jesuits, the Kalispel Indians were giving up their independence to hunt and forage on the land.

The tribe decided to move to a site south of Flathead Lake on common ground where gaming and trading were previously held. Others had succumbed to the white man's alcohol. The Kalispel were in a quandary about living free living at St. Ignatius. They struggled to make ends meet. Chief Victor and the majority of his band moved, instead to the new St. Ignatius Mission location Montana Territory, in 1855.

As miners arriving on Indian land by the thousands, the Walla-Walla went to war on both sides of the Cascades. The Hudson Bay Company qu selling guns and ammunition to the Indians. There was a plot by them to kill the governor. He left the area, making it safely to Olympia and closed the area miners, missionaries and settlers. Other Indians were at risk of being mistaken for the warring Walla-Walla. On May 29, 1855, Agent Isaac Stevens met with the Nez Perce, Umatilla, Cayuse, Walla-Walla and Yakima Indians, but not the Kalispel (Pend Oreille Indians). Stevens sent Lansdale to meet with the Kalispel Indians. Lansdale was to offer these Indians monies to purchase land and place them on a reservation, but was told they had left for the Montana Flathead Reservation and could not be reached.

During the ten years the Jesuits spent with the Kalispel Indian management of their welfare went from the U.S. Army to the Interi Department. After that it was put in the hands of civilians. Indian Agent Lansdale held treaty councils with Chief Victor and the Kalispel Indians during the winter of 1855, at St. Ignatius.

The Kalispel Indians were asked to cede their land. In return, the would receive $40,000 over a twenty year period. In addition, they would receive an agricultural school, grist mill, hospital and a physician, saw mill shops, teachers for black smith, carpenter, farming and other trades. After weighing the situation,

Chief Victor countered with their own offer of one half of the land being generous keeping the land north and east of the Pend' Oreille River and deeding the government the land south and west of the river. The problem w they did not have a bargaining chip. Agent Lansdale said that he did not have t power to change the drafted treaty. Michel's brother, Simon spoke and begged for mercy from the "big father." Matthew spoke and pled for guns an ammunition to hunt and feed the tribe. He said that they had no cattle, horses pigs and could not eat gunpowder.

Victor said the land was not for sale. Hoecking convinced the Kalispel to live on the reserve and retain the homeland. Chief Victor made a proposal They elected to cede half of their land and keep the land north and east of the river and thought this was a fair offer. He would be glad if the "big father," gave his red children a piece of land in their country.

On March 24, 1856, Agent Lansdale arranged for a council at S Ignatius Mission. Michel, a blind Flathead Indian, acted as interpreter. Seven prominent Pend d' Oreille headmen attended. Lansdale, who had become agent for the Flathead tribe, conducted the treaty council.

On Governor Stevens' terms, the Pend Oreille Indians were to cede their lands and go onto the Flathead Reservation in Montana territory. In return, they were to receive a $40,000 dollar grant over a twenty year period, also they were to receive a hospital and physician, a grist mill, blacksmith shop to make guns, plows and wagons, carpentry shop with teachers, and an agricultural-industrial school, with instructors and be taught to farm.

With miners arriving on Indian land by the thousands, the Walla-Walla went to war on both sides of the Cascades. The Hudson Bay Company quit selling guns and ammunition to the Indians. There had been a plot by them to kill the governor. At that time, Governor Stevens left the area, making it safely to Olympia, closing the area to miners, missionaries and settlers. The Salish cousins of the Pend Oreille Indians were warring, but they remained neutral. Settlers had been killed and there had been a threat on the governor's life. Stevens closed the interior for settlement by settlers, traders and missionaries. Hudson's Bay Company discontinued sales of firearms to the Indians.

There were bad feelings among neighboring tribes. Their young men wanted war. On May 6, 1858 Steptoe, five officers and 152 enlisted men crossed the Snake River. Stevens had told the Kalispel that they would be notified of any militia entering their territory. The Pend Oreille marched toward Canada and onto the buffalo plain. 40 Indians attacked surrounding Steptoe's forces. Steptoe retreated. They stole the Army supply train and 100 pack mules. The general had a loss.

The warring Indians did not attack trading posts or missions, but the settlers were not safe in Indian Territory. The Spokane warriors invited the Pend Oreille to join them in war. The Pend Oreille Indians were peacemakers and turned them down. The Walla-Walla Indians were at war on both sides of the Cascades.

The Kalispel Indians were at risk, possibly being mistaken for warring Walla-Walla Indians, who were killing miners and settlers.

Two strike forces under Major Garnett of Fort Simcoe and Colonel Wright of Fort Walla-Walla rode down on the Coeur d'Alene, and a few Pend Oreille Indians. The Spokane prepared for war. Young spirited Pend d' Oreille rode to join them.

PEND D'OREILLE MISSION IN THE ROCKY MOUNTAINS IN 1862.

#37. 1862 Pend d' Oreille Mission Society)

#38. Salish Indians and Sturgeon-nosed Canoe/Courtesy Azusa Publishing, LLC

THE RESERVATION

In 1914, the Kalispel Indians received 4500 acres for a reservation at Usk, Washington in the eastern part of the state. Members of the tribe continued to travel to Idaho, until that slowed, around 1930, continuing their seasonal activities. The Kalispel Indian Reservation is arrowhead shaped and located directly above the Flathead Indian Reservation in present day Montana, bordering now-Idaho, near Missoula on the Canadian Border. A town in Montana was named Kalispel. The Pend d' Oreille share the Flathead Indian Reservation in Montana. The Kalispel Indian Reservation lies north-northwest of Newport, Washington in Pend d' Oreille Country. The reserve is 7.274 square miles, west of the Washington-Idaho border, on the Pend d' Oreille River. The Kalispel casino in Spokane, in Airway Heights on 49.12 acres is the Northern Qwest Casino, operated by the Kalispel tribe.

#39. Salish Village in the Pacific Northwest
(Courtesy of Azusa Publishing)

#40. Wild Trout, food source of the Kalispel Indians
(Author photo)

Chapter Six
KUTENAI INDIANS

The Kutenai spelled (Kootenai or Ktunaxa) is pronounced .tu'nae.hae/ in English. The Kootenai language stock was known as the itunahan. It is an isolated language. There were two dialects of the Kutenai nguage stock, Upper and Lower Kutenai. The Kutenai speech is sing-song, ith musical tones, using an upward inflection at the end of the sentence. Both the dialects contained borrowed words from the Salish language.

The aboriginal Kutenai Indians were divided into two distinct groups, e their language, the Upper and Lower Kutenai of the Plateau. The Upper utenai ranged from Canada down into Montana, between the Rockies and the lkirk Range. The Upper Kutenai dwelled along the Upper Columbia and pper Kootenay Rivers. The Lower Kutenai were associated with the Lower ootenay River drainage. The ancestral home of the Kutenai Indians was the utenai Valley.

Kutenai (Kootenai or Kootenay) Indians of now Southeastern British olumbia, Montana and Idaho were called the Skalzi, lake or water people by eir Salishan neighbors. They did not build totems or have societies. Males ere tall and muscular and the females comely, making up an intelligent race, milar to the Nez Perce. Tribal enemies of the Kutenai were the Assiniboine, lackfoot, Cree and Sarsi.

BUFFALO-HORSE TRADITION

The buffalo hunt to the Upper Missouri is much the same as other bes. The Plains Indian and the horse go together. The Kutenai acquired the rse early and were actually more oriented to the Great Plains tradition and ved in teepees. They developed a horse culture, which offered a means of ealth. The Kutenai Indians were known for their horsemanship skills. Once, arriors of the Plains, the Upper Kutenai hunted the buffalo east of the Rocky ountains. They were a Plains Indian buffalo-horse people who were forced in e early 1800's to retreat onto the Plateau region of the Rocky Mountains by the lackfoot Indians, but lived on both sides of the Continental Divide. The utenai Indians have always been pacifists and not disposed to war.

There was division within the Kutenai Tribe. The Upper Kutenai ntinued the buffalo-horse tradition, hunting bison on the Horse Plains in what now Montana. They were semi-sedentary and adapted to fishing, hunting and raging for food. They were well known for their handcrafted sturgeon nosed noes. They chose to live in the region now known as Idaho.

#41 Kutenai Indian rush gatherer. #42. Kutenai Indian hunts ducks.
(Courtesy Azusa Publishing LLC)

The Upper Kutenai are sometimes classified as Mountain Plains Indians. They allied with the Flathead, Pend d' Oreille and Nez Perce Indians, for their own safety. They returned in one large band to the Plains to hunt buffalo in the autumn on an extended hunt. Communal Kutenai scouts sought out a buffalo herd on horseback by forming a huge circle, with riders spaced far apart. When a herd was located, they signaled the other Indians. First selecting the prime bison, they began the hunt. On the return trip, the horse- mounted Kutenai led pack animals laden with bison meat and robes.

The Upper Kutenai were Mountain Plains Indians and retained the Plains tradition. They adopted the Sun Dance culture and costume, associated with the northern Plains Indians. The Kutenai lived in buffalo skin teepees. The teepee walls were decorated with mystical animal designs. Kutenai Indian garb was adapted from the Plains Indians. Men wore buckskin shirts, breech-clouts, leggings and moccasins and adorned their heads with feathers. Full eagle feather headdresses (war-bonnets) were earned and proudly worn. The women wore deer-skin dresses, knee length leggings, moccasins and fur hats. They wore scanty clothing in the summer.

Tiny seed beads adorned their clothing and moccasins, after the Hudson's Bay Company arrived. Faces were often painted for medicinal purposes or war. Tattooing was common, as well as skin piercing of the ear, lip and nose for jewelry. They traded for shells from the Pacific Coast to make gorgeous earrings.

THE LOWER KUTENAI

The Kootenai people have many explanations for the name, Kutenai. Two translations are "flat-bow people," and "people of the lake." The Plains Indians called them "fish-eaters." Early cave paintings offer no clue to connect the tribe. Their language was not recorded, but they used universal sign language.

Kutenai Indians were matrilocal in times past. The new husband lived with the bride's parents. They lived in the mother's territory and wealth was passed down through the mother's line. In prehistoric times a village had a chief, a sub-chief and wise-men of the tribe. The wise men made up the tribal council. A man's behavior and merit among the people gave him recognition. He had powers linking to the creator and the sun, moon and stars. It was important that he be able to lead men on a hunt or to count coup, by stealing horses. It was essential to have showed bravery on the battle field. A man did not attain the rank of chief until he was an old and wise elder. If he was of good leadership quality, he might be chosen. Their sociopolitical activities had group leaders. There was a band leader, hunt leader (deer-hunt, duck-hunt), fishing leader and war leader, etc. They were polygamous. The Kutenai at one time had slaves. If a warrior exhibited spiritual powers, he became a sub-chief, chief or medicine man.

Another person of high rank in the village was the shaman (medicine man). He had much influence and control over the people. He was highly respected in the tribe. The medicine man was often feared and respected. He was believed to have powers from the spirit world. The shaman was also a spiritual healer and was a powerful shaman, who influenced the hunt and other important matters, having magical powers of healing. He might be asked to lead a "Sun Dance," a ritual acquired from the Plains.

Only a few women attained the rank of "medicine woman." There is a story of a Nez Perce medicine woman, named Elizabeth. When the Nez Perce warriors rode to hunt buffalo, only the elderly, women and children remained. Suddenly, the village was surrounded by Blackfoot warriors. Everyone was frightened. Elizabeth's guardian spirit was thunder. She called on her spirit to save them. Lightning bolts came down. Thunder rolled out of the sky and torrents of rain. The Blackfoot Indians feared the storm and retreated.

When a young man reached maturity the medicine man escorted him into the woods, so he could seek his spirit guide. In the same manner, a medicine woman would escort a young woman. They were left there for a few days to find their spirit and were expected to pick berries or find their food. When a vision or dream came to the young person, their feat was over. A charm might be retained to remember the occasion. The candidate now had spiritual powers and was expected to do well in life. The nature of the event was not to be repeated or they would lose their spirit.

Indian children were taught the way of life by their elders. It was usually the grandparents who educated the children... They told them stories. The grandmothers taught the girls to gather food and cook. She instructed them on how to make baskets and clothing. Grandfather taught the young boys to shoot the bow and arrow and to hunt. The old ones explained to them the customs, religion and traditions. Old men taught the boys to farm. Grandfather normally picked the name for the child, unless the parents had already done so. After the Christian influence, a man took his father's first name as his surname. The young woman did the same, taking her father's first name as her last name.

THE SEASONAL MIGRATION

The lower Kutenai Indians dwelled in very tip of what is now the Idaho panhandle along the Kootenay River drainage and near Lake Pend d' Oreille. The Lower Kutenai were primarily "salmon fishermen" and nomadic "hunters and gatherers." The Lower Kutenai were also hunters and gatherers, like most Indian tribes. The heavily forested mountainous region teemed with flora and fauna. Before the hunt, a religious ceremony was held. The people chanted, danced and sang. All this was to celebrate for a good hunt. During the spring cycle the Lower Kutenai Indian men hunted and fished and the women foraged. The women dug roots. while the men hunted bear, beaver, deer, marmot and occasionally, buffalo. The Kutenai Indians subsisted on fish, roots and game. They were a semi-sedentary group in the Plateau culture. Roots, pine-moss and wild onions were cooked along with the meat for flavor. The berries, nuts and seeds were gleaned by the women. They picked blackberries, blueberries, choke-cherries, huckleberries, service-berries and thorn-berries. The women also trapped small mammals.

The Kutenai River empties into the Columbia River, which ran to the ocean. In the spring, the fish hunters migrated to fishing camps on the river, where salmon were bountiful. Sometimes, the ladies participated in fishing activities. Thousands of salmon flourished and migrated upstream to spawn in the Kutenai River. Wild fish caught were bull trout, cutthroat trout, kokanee salmon, rainbow trout and mountain whitefish. The Kutenai Indians used to trap fish. They built v-shaped stone dams, called weirs that reached across the river about three feet in height to slow the fish enough to spear them with a harpoon and line. A major portion of their diet was made up of native fish caught in the Kootenai River. Fish were baked, boiled, broiled or smoked. Some were sun-dried and preserved in cedar box bins.

The Kutenai became fishers and developed fishing camps. A fishing headman was chosen and teepees were pitched in a circle for security. Baskets were also used to trap and catch fish. Tule reeds were bundled and used to construct rafts. Rivers were full to overflowing in the spring, with fish in the sloughs and ponds with traps set to catch them. In the camp there was much storytelling, chanting and dancing to the music and the drums. The complete fishing complex was shrouded with religious overtones of good fortune and a good catch. The Kutenai chief normally presided over gathering and distributing the fish in the village, which were collected in baskets or bark boxes and divided among all of the families, distributed by young boys. Women prepared the fish before lowering them in water filled cooking baskets, heated by red hot stones.

In the summer cycle the women picked bitterroot and dug camas and scores of other roots for sustenance. The camas was baked in underground fire pits, either stored for winter or pounded into flour in mortars to make "camas bread." Kutenai women used baskets to carry berries, nuts, roots and seeds. Food was stored underground in baskets inside of cedar boxes and covered with earth and boughs. Kutenai Indians cached berries, dried fish, jerked meat and roots in baskets to be stored underground for winter. Pemmican was jerked meat or fish pounded fine in a mortar and pestle and mixed with melted fat made into cakes, with choke-cherries or berries, and cached for the winter. Fishing lasted through the summer and continued into the autumn season.

Seeds and berries were picked and roots dug in autumn. In autumn the Kutenai Indians held communal deer drives, which resembled the communal bison drive. Deer were in abundance providing a constant food source. A deer hunt leader was elected, who led the excursion. Drives were held by encircling the deer, trapping them in netting in the center and slaughtering them.

The Kutenai Indians didn't make pottery, but excelled in basket making. "Digging sticks" were employed to dig a variety of roots, which were made from a branch with antler handles and a fire hardened point. Elk horn was also used for digging.

The winter cycle involved hunters taking large game, some fishing and use of berries, jerked meat, roots, and other foods, which were stored. They also grew tobacco. The balance of the year was spent hunting game. The mountains were rich in bear (brown, black and grizzly), bighorn sheep, caribou, cougar, deer, ducks, elk, fox, geese, grouse, ptarmigan and mountain goats. Natural resources in their environment provided a substantial diet.

Wild fish caught in the Kootenay River drainage were bull trout, cutthroat trout, rainbow trout, mountain white fish, and the white sturgeon. During salmon season, they had a fishing camp... Salmon fishing was their main industry. A spot where fishing was best was chosen. When the kokanee and Chinook salmon fought their way upstream to spawn, the Kutenai Indians harvested the bounty. They employed baskets, bow and arrows, gaffs, harpoons and spears to catch salmon. Salmon were dried in the sunlight and stacked in piles and stored for winter. Salmon fillets, fat and berries were ground in mortar and pestles. The result was made into cakes and stored in salmon skins, called pemmican, stored for winter in underground pits.

The Kutenai Indians used fire heated stones that were transferred to earthen pots, containing water for cooking. Meat was boiled, also in birch bark bowls and water tight baskets. One basket that they made was a water tight basket of split reeds and could be used to boil meat, using fire heated stones. This was a custom of the Plains Indians. When the Hudson's Bay Company arrived, they introduced iron kettles to the Kutenai Indians. The sturdy iron kettle added one more means of using the fire heated stone method of cooking for the Kutenai Indians. Three flat stones, called fire dogs, supported an earthen pot or iron kettle on a fire. Fowl or rabbit was cooked on a spit or roasted on a stick over a fire. Earthen ovens were used to bake bread or cook pine nuts and camas tubers.

Meat was jerked for winter. Furs were tanned for blankets, clothing and moccasins. Skins made teepee coverings. Deerskin made fine clothing. Kutenai Indian women were skilled craftsmen. They made teepee skins and decorated them with ornate designs. They made shirts, leggings, skirts and loin cloths of deerskin. Sandals, moccasins, fur gloves and caps were all made by hand. Blankets were constructed of rabbit fur.

Ornate baskets were woven from birch branches and wild cherry roots, which they were used in cooking, fishing and food storage. Tight woven baskets held water. Baskets were used as containers for berries, roots, seeds, and jerked meat. Pottery was traded in. Foods were stored in pottery, baskets or bark boxes. Apparently the clay on Kutenai ground was unsuitable for pottery. Platters were made from moose bone and spoons from deer antler. Paint was made from clay, mixed with animal fat or fish oil. This paint was used on their faces and other parts of the body. Fruit juices and minerals, mixed made paint for baskets and other uses.

Tools and weaponry of the Kutenai were standard fishing tools. They utilized the stone hammer, tomahawk, or war club, stone knives, and hide scrapers. Arrow heads were tooled from chert, flint or obsidian.

Sports in prehistoric days included foot races. They loved games played with sticks and game-stones. Horse racing was a favorite event.

After the Hudson's Bay Company and other trading companies arrived, bright colored glass beads became available. Ceremonial and dance costumes were very decorative. The Indians adorned their clothing with colored beads and painted their bodies. Feathered headdresses were worn.

The Kutenai Indians grew a small amount of tobacco for their pipes, which were made of clay or stone. They smoked the American tobacco root or red kinninickinnik, a mixture of bark, leaves and tobacco.

Two types of canoes were constructed. The dugout canoe was crafted from a large tree trunk, and had the famous sturgeon nose. The other type of canoe was the birch bark canoe. This canoe was tricky to navigate and balance. The two types of canoe were utilized for transportation and fishing. The Kutenai Indians paddled their sturgeon nosed canoes barefoot. They often fished and walked in marshes with no moccasins and were known by some tribes as "bare footed Indians."

KUTENAI HOUSES

Kutenai Indian houses were a dome shaped willow structure, covered with reed or rush matting. They acquired the horse and had skin teepees, a tradition learned from the Plains. Teepees were more a summer hut. The sweat lodge was built like a dome shaped willow hut and covered with skins. A sweat lodge was a sociopolitical affair for the men. Sometimes both sexes bathed at once. Four or five bathers could partake at once. They could talk about everything that was going on in their village. A fire was built in the middle of the room. Several stones were placed in the fire. When the stones were red hot, water was poured on the glowing stones, producing steam. The sweat lodge was religious as well as a social occasion. Petitions to their creator were said, accompanied with chanting, for good fortune and to free them of ailments and disease. After enjoying the steam bath the Indians ran down and plunged into a cold river. The sweat bath was a health measure and the Kutenai believed that it rid them of evil demons.

They had birthing huts and menstrual huts. Birthing huts were used for pregnant women and menstrual huts during their menstrual cycle. Sometimes these huts were combined. At the first sign of puberty, the girl was ushered into seclusion. The grandmother or mother attended the young woman at the time. A cleansing ritual was performed. Her family had to keep her isolated. If the purification was not done properly, harm might befall her. The expectant mother was careful not to wear any tight cords or necklaces, which might hurt the baby. Superstition and fear surrounded childbirth. When a baby was born it was a maternal affair. Bad spirits were dealt with to keep them away from the mother and child. Older women watched over the young mothers in childbirth. They stayed in the hut one month.

RELIGION

Their religion entailed animism and sun worship. The Kutenai believe in one creator above all of the spirits. He was supernatural and in contact with mankind. He helped them but was offended by man's wrong-doing. He withdrew to another place and only contacted man through the sun, moon and stars. No Indian was worthy to come in contact with him. They called their god "Nupeeks."

The Kutenai Indians were superstitious about the dead and never spea the spoke of the departed. A dead person was held upright and the whole band would pass by and shake the hand of the deceased. The body was washed and dressed for burial. A blanket was sewn around the cadaver, covering the head. The body was placed on a platform for one day, then lifted down and buried. Death was clouded by superstition. There was mourning and wailing for the dead. If a chief died the whole band would move to a new campsite. The new chief secured a new campsite on high ground, near water and firewood.

The Kutenai's celebrated the coming of the New Year with a dance. their religion dances were important. The dance was supposed to benefit the people preparing them for the "Happy Earth," (their heaven). In order to have good year, they received blessings from the spirits and people that had passed, have a good coming year.

#43. Kutenai Mother and Papoose in Village Scene (Courtesy of the Idaho State Historical Society)

Kutenai mother child in cradleboard and chief- (Courtesy of the Idaho State Historical Society)

The dance is called the "Winter Spirit Dance." In this dance, the medicine man entered in between the spirits and the people, to give them powers. During the dance, the people would stand in the dance circle with one person holding the wishing rod in his hand, starting a line. He would chant and begin the dance and the other dancers would follow. The line dance moved all around the circle several times, as the leader chanted. The other dancers chanted with him. Singers chanted and wailed to the music, as dancers moved slowly and rhythmically to the beat of the tom-tom. Maybe a bone flute accompanied the music or a wooden mariachi. Both sexes danced, but usually alone. The men danced in one circle, the women in another.

The Kutenai loved to hear and tell stories. Tales were told to the young and old. Illustrations of mythical animated characters were told. Animal heroes enacted life dramas, both humorous and fascinating. Using magic these heroes could change into another character or bring a hero, who had died, back to life.

WHITE MEN AND THE KUTENAI

The French traders called the Kutenai Indians "Arezaplats," meaning anglicized Flat-bows. The Kutenai Indians encountered the Hudson's Bay Company, when David Thompson contacted them and built trading posts in their vicinity, as early as 1780. Many fur traders chose Indian brides. The only women near them were Indians, so many took Indian brides, but seldom did these unions work. The Jesuits advised against such marriages.

Father De Smet observed the Kutenai Fish Festival, when the season ended, in 1845. The Indians were visited on a yearly basis by Jesuit missionaries from De Smet in Idaho Territory, who erected a church at the south end of Long Arm Island, to be named Mission Hill. After a few years a second church was built with lumber donated by Bonner Ferry residents.

The Canadian Kutenai, the Upper Pend d' Oreille and the Flathead Tribes signed a treaty with the United States in July of 1855. This land was ceded to the American government in exchange for their reservations. The Kutenai Tribe was not represented and were left without land. Before 1900 white homesteaders chose land in the Kootenai Valley, including village sites. Kutenai Indians were given land allotments to encourage farming, but no reservation was established and they lacked training and capital to farm. Edward Bonner came to Kutenai Indian country in 1863. He purchased the rights to operate a ferry across the Kootenai River from Kutenai Indian Chief Abraham. It became known as Bonner's Ferry.

While Thomas Blind was chief, in the late 1800's, the Kootenai dwelt in teepees, however they lacked a reservation home. Chief Blind chose a village site

#45. Cheyenne Sun Dancers
The Kutenai Indian Sun Dance was copied from the Plains Indians.
(Photograph Courtesy AZUSA PUBLISHING, LLC)

three miles below Bonners Ferry south of the Kootenai River. When Chief Blind passed in 1869, his son became chief. As was the custom, he moved the village upon the death of a chief. Chief Abraham Blind moved the village just west of the trading post. He built the first Kutenai "log cabin" and convinced others to do the same. Five cabin homes were built there in 1887. Abraham died in 1887, so sub Chief Isaac Adams moved the village one and one half miles farther west.

The American government urged the Kutenai Indians to take up farming. It was during this time that the Indians tried to form a dike and drainage district to avoid flooding. For lack of funds many just sold their lands rather than experience a hassle. Many of them wound up working on the ranches. From 1800 into the 1900's, the Kutenai population had been reduced in size by one half from white man's cholera and smallpox. In 1885, in an agreement arranged by the U.S. Government, Kutenai Chief Moses invited the Chief Joseph band of Nez Perce to come and live on the Colville Reservation.

Jesuit Priests recommended that the band remain in place after the death of a chief. By doing this, they would not lose their land to settlers. If they remained in the location, the teepee had to be moved to rid it of evil spirits. The grandmother was summoned, to rid the teepee of malicious apparitions. Cedar boughs were cut and piled on the bed of the deceased and it was burned. The chief's body was washed well and dressed. Everyone in the band walked by and said goodbye. The body was sewn into a blanket, around a pole for burial. The pall bearers would lift the pole to their shoulders and carry the body to the grave. The practice was discontinued. The belongings of the deceased were given away, except for a few personal mementos for the family. The custom of giving was shown in an old folk tale of a chief, who poured a large bag of arrowheads on a mountainside. Warriors could go there and find flint to make arrowheads.

THE RESERVATION

Kutenai tribal members were urged to move to the Montana Flathead Reservation in 1855. They did not like the idea at first, as they enjoyed the freedom to hunt and fish. They refused to go. Few families were to move onto the reservation from 1895-1910. The government gave them a land allotment in 1895. They still had no tribal agency. The Indian Council gave every family 80 acres of land. Five or so acres were cleared and they farmed the land. Fruits and vegetables were raised, as well as chickens, hogs and horses. Hay was put up to feed the cattle. Eventually, most tribal members were relocated to the Flathead Indian Reservation in Montana. Some were forced to move. The majority adapted to reservation life, worked hard and adjusted well. Today many are successful. They hold onto their heritage and culture.

The Flathead Indian Reservation covers 1.3 million acres in western Montana. The reservation lies on the southern end of Flathead Lake, which is the largest lake in the western United States, once called Salish Lake. The reservation lies in forested mountains and valleys, west of the Continental Divide. It takes in parts of Flathead Lake, Missoula and Sanders counties.

The Indians on the Flathead reservation call themselves the onfederated Salish and Kootenai Tribes of the Flathead Nation. The Bitterroot lish, Kootenai and Pend d' Oreille Indian Tribes, also reside there. The servation was created from the 1855 Hell gate Treaty. The total number of dians that live there was 26,172 at the time of the 2,000 census. The largest mmunity on the reservation is the town of Polson, Montana.

The Flathead government first organized under the Indian eorganization Act of 1936. There is a ten member tribal council and the seat of e tribal government is at Pablo, Montana. The tribal government provides the ajority of jobs on the reservation, as well as a number of services. The Salish ootenai College and the People's Center Museum are operated by the tribes, as ell as. It is self governing and a member of the American Indian Higher ducation Consortium.

The Kootenay Indian Reservation is in Boundary County, Idaho, 25 iles south of the Canadian border, 1.9 miles west-northwest of Bonners Ferry. ne reservation covers 17.922 acres. The 2,000 census population was 75 ople. Never having signed a treaty, the tribe declared war on the United ates.

KUTENAI MYTHOLOGY

A Kutenai tale was told about a medicine man, named Raven. He led s men in battle against the enemy. Raven circled their foes and they fired their eapons at him, but the bullets bounced off his garment and fell on the ground. 's warriors picked them up and reloaded, firing at the enemy. The medicine an repeated this several times. Raven had used his powers to win the battle.

One Kutenai story was how Marten got his spots. Marten and Mink ere brothers. Mink was the elder and took care of Marten. He told Marten ways to stay close to their home and not wander. Marten began wondering nat was over the hill, so he climbed all of the way to the top. In a valley below saw a teepee and Mrs. Bear, working in her yard. She went back into the epee. Marten followed her. He sat across from her and she offered him a bowl pemmican. When he reached over the fire for the bowl, she grabbed his arm d pulled him into the fire. Marten jumped up from the fire and ran all the way me and hid in a blanket. When Mink came home, he found Marten there. arten told him the story of events. Marten's fur was burned in several places, he dressed the wounds. They still scarred. That is how Martens got their ots.

Another story is how Owl got his wide eyes. He spent much of his time ing in a tall tree. Owl had a friend, Mouse. They liked to play together. One ght Owl sat high in his tree and Mouse called to him to come and play. Owl s fast asleep and did not hear him. Just then Snake slithered up to Mouse, o saw him and screamed at the top of his lungs. Owl woke with a start, but it s too late. Snake had swallowed Mouse. Owl was so surprised that he opened eyes wider and wider. That is how Owl got his big wide eyes.

The Kutenai Indians tell another story of a brave seeking a spirit guide. Long, long ago a boy named Lassaw climbed to the top of a mountain. He fasted there for two days and nights. Somehow Lassaw injured his finger. He tore his shirt and bandaged the wound. The finger throbbed, so he prayed to the Great Spirit for help. Suddenly, Lassaw saw a buffalo drinking water. It quenched its thirst and looked at Lassaw and spoke to him in the Kutenai tongue. "I know that you are hurt. I came to help you. Whatever you ask, I will give you," the buffalo said, and then vanished. He had found his spirit guide and knew that the buffalo would always be with him. Lassaw became a great buffalo hunter and lived a happy life. These stories were told and retold in the tribe.

Chapter Seven
NEZ PERCE INDIANS

The Nez Perce Indians were in one place for thousands of years. They fished in the Snake River region of Hell's Canyon and dwelled in present day northern Idaho, Oregon and Washington. The Nez Perce, Palouse and Spokane Indians were all sedentary fishermen in the prehistoric days. The area teemed with bighorn sheep, bear, cougar, deer and elk which provided good hunting. Salmon runs provided a wealth of fish to fill the belly and to store in bundled cakes for winter. Recently, an ancient fishing village has been found in Hell's Canyon by archeologists. The Wallowa Nez Perce of today gather yearly for a Friendship Feast and Powwow, as did their ancestors in ancient days.

The Nez Perce (the Chutepula tribe) called themselves the "Nee-Me-Poo" or "the people." The Nez Perce Tribe in their tongue was "Chutepula." The Nez Perce language spoken language is Nimipuutimpt. Their language comes from the Plateau Penutian linguistic stock. Neighboring tribes, the Klamath, Umatilla and Yakima Indians spoke different dialects of the Sahaptian language. Trade was established among Columbia River and Coastal Indians communicated by sign language. The Nez Perce were a civilized people and an intelligent race. The men were handsome, six foot in stature and their women fair.

It is estimated that the Nez Perce became horse people around 1700. They most probably traded for their first horses and acquired Appaloosa horses from the Comanche Indians or their Shoshoni cousins at their trade center. The Nez Perce and Palouse people were culturally linked. They bred and raised the splendid Appaloosa horse. Over time their herds numbered in the thousands. It was no rare sight to see the Nez Perce trailing four hundred mounts to the Shoshoni trade fair. Not only were they excellent horse handlers, but they were of the finest horsemen among the Plains Indians.

The name, "Appaloosa," for the gorgeous spotted horse, probably came from the tribe that raised them, the Palouse. The Palouse either got the horse from the Shoshoni or the Nez Perce. The name "Palouse," could have come from French fur trappers. Palouse Country evolved from the same origin, also the slang word, Appalousey, referred to the horse. In America, in 1938, Appaloosa became its official name.

In 1800, the Nez Perce Country ranged over about seventeen million acres that would become Idaho, Oregon and Washington. The area reached from the Bitterroot Mountains to the Blue Mountain Range. In 1805, the Nez Perce made up the largest tribe in the Columbia River Plateau, with a population of about 6,000 Native Americans in 300 camps and villages. The tribe was a peaceful one. They bred beautiful Appaloosa horses and other breeds that they had obtained from the Comanche and Shoshoni Indians. The Nez Perce hunted, fished for salmon and dug camas bulbs. They lived in extended families in villages.

The heavy rock writing in Hell's Canyon is evidence of their habitation. Hundreds of ancient petro-glyphs appear along the Snake River, on Hell's Canyon's rock and walls. They traded at the fur forts for woven blankets, metal kettles, tobacco, knives and guns. When hundreds of trappers, missionaries and settlers moved into Nez Perce country, half of the Indian populations died of diseases contracted from them.

LEWIS AND CLARK VISIT THE NEZ PERCE

The Nez Perce Indians were contacted by the Spanish explorers, and later, Lewis and Clark. The Lewis and Clark Expedition arrived in Nez Perce country to build additional dugout canoes. This site was called "Canoe Camp." Trees were felled along the river for dugout canoes, fashioned from logs as needed. When they contacted the Indians, they found them scantily dressed. The Indians befriended Lewis and Clark. They smoked the pipe with them. The Nez Perce gave them food, shelter and horses. They lavished gifts on them. .

Lewis and Clark first sat down on a blanket to trade with the Nez Perce in 1805. The Nez Perce told them they did not want red beads, but preferred blue ones. Early on, Spanish explorers brought glass beads for trade with the Indians, to their delight. They called the pale blue donut shaped bead of the Spanish "a piece of the sky." This was living proof that Spanish conquistadors made contact with the Nez Perce, early. The explorers, Lewis and Clark heard blue padres called tia com-mo-shack, in the Nez Perce language, meaning "chief of all beads." The tribe held the party's horses as they crossed the Rocky Mountains, until their return. They found passage through the Rocky Mountains, by canoeing the Clearwater River to the Snake River and then on to the Columbia and the Pacific Ocean. In 1818, an agreement between America and Great Britain was made where Indian land was shared with whites. The Bureau of Indian Affairs was created in 1824.

Marcus and Narcissa Prentiss Whitman with Henry and Eliza Spalding traveled overland from New York, reaching Fort Boise in 1836. Whitman's was the first wagon to cross the plains. The broken down remnant was abandoned at the old fort. The party was escorted on to "Fort Vancouver" by Hudson's Bay Company employees. Narcissa and Eliza were the first white women in Oregon. In 1836 Reverend Henry Spalding built his Presbyterian Mission School at Lapwai on Nez Perce ground. It was 12 miles north of Lewiston, on the Clearwater River. The Mission was Idaho's first settlement. He imported a printing press to print the New Testament in the Nez Perce language. The same year Marcus Whitman established the Whitman Presbyterian Mission on Cayuse ground, near thousands of Indians, who lived 25 miles east of Fort Walla-Walla. He also established another mission at Kamiah, 50 miles northeast of Lapwai.

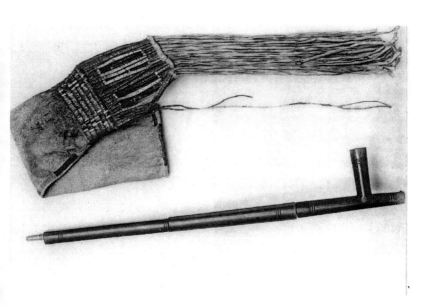

#46. Calumet Bag and Pipe-The Nez Perce sat down and smoked
the peace pipe with Lewis and Clark.
(Courtesy of the Idaho State Historical Society)

#47. The buffalo was at the top of the food chain.
It was the Plains Indians' most important resource.
Hunting buffalo with the horse was practical. (Author Photo)

Whitman and Spalding brought wagon loads of supplies to their missions from Green River, Wyoming, establishing a wagon route to Fort Walla-Walla. Rev. Whitman promised the Cayuse Indians monies for land that was never paid. When the Foreign Missions Board closed the Oregon Missions on October 1843, Whitman started back East, crossed the Blue Mountains and joined a trading company, en route to St. Louis.

Whitman arrived to seek monies, but was refused. He sold his home to raise the money. Whitman left New York on horseback, with pack animals. He reached the Platte River country in Nebraska. There in 1843. Marcus Whitman joined emigrants bound for Fort Walla-Walla and headed up a massive wagon-train into Oregon Hundreds followed. Dr. Whitman wrote to James Porter, Secretary of War, saying he had piloted one thousand settlers with 120 wagons, 700 oxen and 800 cattle to Oregon in 1843. They stopped at Fort Boise and purchased coffee and flour from the Hudson Bay's Company at $50 dollars per hundred weight, spending $2,000.00, a good price.

In Whitman's absence, Cayuse Indians attacked the mission, burned down a grist mill and other buildings, as the Nez Perce demonstrated at Lapwai. Mrs. Whitman fled to Fort Walla-Walla. Agent White spoke to the Cayuse and continued on to Lapwai to parley with the Nez Perce, smoke the pipe and sign a peace treaty. An Infantry Regiment was assigned to the Northwest.

Hundreds of pioneers came to the Whitman Mission. Some had the dreaded measles. Cayuse Indians were stricken by the epidemic and knew the source. Whitman warned them against it, but they bathed in cold water to combat the high fever. They died as a result.

As the Whitman's attended the sick, November 29, 1847, a Cayuse War-Party ambushed them, killing Reverend and Mrs. Whitman and eleven others. Two lay dying. Women and children were taken hostage. Thirteen escaped. Some reached Lapwai Mission, others Fort Vancouver. During the time of the massacre Nez Perce Indians harbored Dr. and Mrs. Spalding, saving their lives.

The mission was closed down. The Cayuse War began in 1847, which set a precedent of Indian wars in the Pacific Northwest for the next 50 years. A civilian, Cornelius Gilliam led five hundred settlers in attacks on central Oregon Indian tribes in retaliation for the Whitman's deaths. In the autumn of 1849 the Cayuse Indians turned over five of their tribe, who had been involved in the Whitman Massacre.

YOUNG CHIEF JOSEPH

Old Joseph in his native tongue was called Tuekakas, chief of the allam-wat-kin (Wallowa) band. Old Joseph, the Elder was one of the first nverts to Christianity at the Lapwai Mission.

Reverend Spalding performed the marriage ceremony for Tuekakas and napkhaponimi, his wife. In 1840, a defender of the people was born to them in cave near the Grande Rhonde River. His name was In-mut-too-yah-lat-lat, in e Chutepula (Nez Perce) tongue, meaning Thunder-Traveling-over-the-ountains. His common name was "Young Joseph" (Joseph the Younger). seph was one of seven children. He was baptized, "Ephraim" by Reverend alding. Joseph attended the Spalding Mission School on Lapwai Creek. He ent several years there, before returning to Wallowa in 1847.

In 1855, Governor Isaac I. Stevens gathered the regional Indian chiefs r a treaty council and feast. Old Joseph carried his Bible. They agreed to cede land for a large reservation in Wallowa and coexistence. the Steven's treaty is signed by the Cayuse, Nez Perce, Umatilla and the Walla-Walla, but soon uld be broken. (Halalhot-suut) Lawyer signed, as did (Apash) Looking Glass d reluctantly, Tuekakas.

In 1860, gold was discovered on Nez Perce land. Ten thousand miners d settlers disregarded the treaty and trespassed on lands of the Nez Perce. In 63, the Nez Perce refused to sign a thief and steal treaty. Agents in 1868 manded the Nez Perce leave their scenic Walla-Walla Valley, teeming with eeks, rivers and game with the beautiful Wallowa Mountains in the ckground, for a Lapwai Reservation. Young Joseph and his father fought this ea but Lawyer signed.

Young Joseph was a handsome, stately Nez Perce Indian. He married a z Perce woman, named Wa-win-te-pi-skat, daughter of a chief, called, Whisk-s-ket. (1865) They had a daughter, Kap-kap-on-mi-in.

Old Joseph wouldn't have anything to do with the soldier peace council d stopped his ears to their treaties. He warned Young Joseph not to accept fts from the white man for they might claim the gifts were trade for their land. e also told his son not to give up the land of their fathers. He did not trust yone who would buy and sell land. All of his life, Young Chief Joseph tried to ep his word to his father. The Indians believed that they could not possess the d, but that they were put here to manage the land. After the Great White ther in Washington broke his word, Old Joseph was disgruntled and heart-oken, He disposed of his Bible and American flag.

#48. Unidentified Nez Perce Warriors- about 1860 (Courtesy of Idaho State Historical Society)

#49. Old Nez Perce "Wise One" (Courtesy of Idaho State Historical Society)

At the time Young Joseph's elder brother, Sousouquee was killed by enemy Indians. Young Joseph became the elder brother. Another brother was named Ollokut (Little Frog) who became hunt leader during excursions to follow the buffalo and warrior.

When Young Joseph's father became seriously ill, Joseph took on the duties of peacetime village chief and leader. When Old Joseph died in 1871, Young Joseph expressed his feelings in this poem:

> *I buried him in the valley of the winding waters. (Wallowa)*
> *I love that land more than all the rest of the world.*

After his father's death, Young Joseph became chief of the Wallowa Nez Perce. He stated that a man who would not defend his father's grave is worse than a wild animal. The Nez Perce had been friendly and also fair to the explorers, the fur trappers and to the white settlers. Now, the pendulum was swinging the other way. Many white men were coming. The white man and his armies were pushing them off their lands.

On June 16, 1873, President Grant reserved land in Wallowa Valley for the Nez Perce Indians, led by Chief Joseph. The Nez Perce were promised Wallowa (Winding water in Nez Perce), but white settlers were greedy and wanted the fertile ground. In 1875, Wallowa was opened for white settlement.

In 1876 a commission met with the Nez Perce to offer them to move to the 1863 designated reservation by April 1, 1877. U.S. Army General Oliver O. Howard was placed in command of relocation. General Howard had fought in the Civil War, in Mr. Lincoln's Army. At the Battle of Seven Pines in Virginia, a Minnie ball shattered his right arm, which had to be amputated.

Joseph remarried a woman named, Spring Time, who would bare him another daughter, in 1877. He would take four wives and father nine children and raise some that were orphaned. Joseph said that "it was better to live in peace than to begin a war and lie dead." He and Ollokut agreed to move the Wallowa Band to Lapwai. Chief Joseph became a great orator, statesman and war-chief. Joseph was the noble red man to both Indian and white man and a 'champion of the people." He conceded to the Government to save his people.

The council meeting at Lapwai began on May 2, 1877. Joseph (the orator), narrated the wrongs to his people and the need for them to be treated fairly and said he did not speak with a forked tongue. General Howard urged them to go on the reservation. The government took Joseph's lands, horses and cattle, giving him reasons to rebel. General Howard broke his promise to Chief Joseph, ordering the Nez Perce, with livestock, to be on the reservation in 30 days, and then reordered the soldiers to round up the Indians. General Howard had promised Joseph the Wallowa Valley. The army took over their land.

Chiefs Joseph, White Bird and Too-hul-hut-sote held a council at Lake Tolo at the head of Rocky Canyon. Joseph's first objective was peace but was accused of being a coward. In Rocky Canyon they held festivities with dancing, stick games, horse Races and parades. They took advantage of their freedom at the time.

War-chiefs under Chief Young Joseph were Chiefs Looking Glass, Mox-Mox, Ollokut, Too-hul-hut-sote, White Bird and Yellow Bull. Chief Ollokut was Joseph's brother and the hunt leader during excursions to follow the buffalo. Chief Peo-peo-hi-hi-h translated to White Bird from the Nez Perce Language. White Bird was a shaman and a loyal sub-chief. He was a valiant warrior skilled in Indian warfare. Chief Looking Glass earned his name because of the signal mirror he wore on a leather thong around his neck.

Joseph and Ollokut were absent when unruly braves, who had purchased guns from settlers and drank "firewater." Walaitits, Red Moccasin, and Swan Necklace drank until they were intoxicated, becoming belligerent and readied for war. Walaitits was urged to kill the white eyes who murdered his father. The braves rode to the Salmon River and Slate Creek on June 13, 1877, hid behind rocks and shot Richard Devine in his open doorway. Next, they rode to John Day, killing Robert Bland, Harry Beckroge and Henry Elfers.

When they returned, Chief White Bird mounted his horse and rode through camp, urging war, while his braves made more raids. Toohulhutsote joined them in attacking the whites. He had been jailed by the Army, which fueled the spark that ignited the Nez Perce War. Joseph wanted to return to the reservation and seek peace, as did many of his tribe. Several returned to Lapwai Reservation. Ollokut remained silent. Three Eagles said that he could not go back and vowed to fight. It was too late. The damage had been done. Seventeen white men were killed. The Nez Perce War had begun.

Settlers at Slate Creek heard rumors of Indian war. They readied to fight, with only 23 men, 40 women and children and few firearms. Citizens hurried to build a stockade. They sent someone for help. Tolo (Alanewa), wife of Tawe (Red Wolf), an Indian woman, was elected. Tolo traveled 25 miles to Florence, a mining town, returning with twelve armed miners. A monument near Grangeville was erected in her honor.

WHITE BIRD CANYON

The tribe had to eat so Joseph and his chiefs moved over into White Bird Canyon where they rounded up their cattle for butchering. White Bird Canyon is very grassy with steep rolling hills. The terrain is uneven with buttes, knolls and ridges. The creek runs through the bottom land.

General Howard sent to Fort Vancouver and Fort Walla-Walla for more fighting units which were moved by steamship up river to Nez Perce Country. At Fort Lapwai, troops received rigid training in Indian fighting at Fort Lapwai. On June 15, Captain Perry and two companies from Fort Vancouver arrived at Fort Lapwai. On June 16, He and companies F & H, (a complement of ninety-eight men), left for White Bird Canyon. The soldiers lost sleep, being in the saddle for days. It was drizzling rain, as they rode to Cottonwood and Grangeville. Chief Joseph's scouts observed the procession as they advanced.

The U.S. Cavalry led by Capt. Perry, his militia and scouts arrived in White Bird Canyon about midnight the evening of June 16. At dawn the next day, June 17, 1877, Perry and his two companies, with eleven volunteers and scouts rode down the 3,000 foot descent to creek level. About 300 yards out, troops led by Lieutenant Theller saw six Nez Perce Indians on horseback moving toward them, carrying the white flag of truce. A rifle cracked then another broke the silence. Ad Chapman, Theller's scout, fired two rounds that struck the dirt near the flag bearers. Indian observers scattered on the field, returning fire. Perry's men fired on the Indians and began the clash.

THE NEZ PERCE WAR

The Nez Perce War was underway. Nez Perce warriors stripped down to loin-cloths and moccasins, according to their tradition. Chief Joseph, on the other hand, remained in war-shirt, deerskin leggings, and moccasins. He had no choice but to fight. An old Indian war slogan was, "it is a good day to die."

The Indians began the fighting. Lieutenant Theller and his volunteers attacked. Chief Joseph ordered the horse herd taken down to the river behind the bluff and the women and children broke camp. He divided his forces into two groups under Chiefs Ollokut and Two Moons. They led the charge, attacking from two sides. Joseph blocked attack across the center.

The army had a complete military arsenal at their disposal during this campaign. The Indians had only 50 guns plus bows and arrows, lances, tomahawks and stone knives. Chiefs Too-hul-hut-sote and White Bird fought bravely. The old Indian trick of running horses through the enemy's ranks divided the soldiers. Soon they were in disarray and confused... Horses ran free. Smoke and gunfire filled the air. Rifle cracks came continually. The rancid smell of gunpowder in the air was overpowering.

#50. Chief Joseph at Lapwai with Alice C. Fletcher, Allotting Agent
(Courtesy of Idaho State Historical Society)

#51. The site of White Bird Battlefield, where shots were fired
that started the Nez Perce War. (Author Photo)

The Indians uttered shrill war-cries, causing their horses to spook, so e soldiers had to dismount, causing Perry and his men to retreat. Chief White rd pursued Perry and his men fired on them as they retreated to Cottonwood. hite Bird chased them all the way to Johnson's ranch before turning back. The attle of White Bird Canyon left 33 soldiers dead and seven wounded. Joseph d fewer losses, thus his Nez Perce had the victory, delivering a defeat, second ly to the one at the Little Big Horn. People feared Chief Joseph would nquer Howard and unite with the Columbia Plateau Indians becoming beatable.

Chief Joseph returned to his lodge to learn that he had become father of baby girl. Chief Looking Glass arrived with more warriors. That night the dians held a victory dance. The following day, in a brilliant tactical maneuver, seph exited White Bird Canyon in a wide circle, to make tracking them very fficult. Chief Joseph and nearly 300 warriors pulled up stakes and moved to e Clearwater River, trying to avoid war. The Nez Perce had begun an exodus at would continue for months. The Chief avoided contact with Major Green's ree companies of Cavalry, Buffalo Horn and his twenty Bannock scouts, who ere coming from Fort Boise.

General Howard, with 400 troops and 100 scouts, had left Lake Tolo r Fort Lapwai, on June 22.nd. Howard sent Trimble on June 23rd to Slate Creek defend the citizens. Trimble awaited word of reinforcements from Lewiston, d then pushed his men to overtake the Indians.

On June 25th Howard split his column and advanced to Johnson's nch. He was joined in Grangeville by Captain Perry and his remaining troops. e General arrived at White Bird Canyon on June 26th, to find the rain had ashed the dirt from the shallow graves exposing bodies of dead soldiers. oward had them reburied. The corpses had been stripped of clothing, but seph's warriors had taken no scalps. Captain Paige climbed to the crest of a gh ridge and from that viewpoint he surveyed the Indians, beyond the Salmon ver who were, retreating. Captain Miles and his men arrived at White Bird.

General Howard, 700 Cavalry, Buffalo Horn and 20 Bannock scouts rsued the Nez Perce, on June 28. Joseph crossed the Salmon River baiting the eneral, in order to cut off his supply lines. Five Wounds and Rainbow mained behind, with other snipers, to slow Howard's progress taking pot-shots the soldiers approaching the crossing. Soldiers returned fire with long rifles, the Indians disappeared.

Joseph's people had crossed the river with little trouble; Howard had a ugh time crossing with all the big guns and supply wagons. Joseph re-crossed e river at Craig's Ferry and attacked Howard from the rear causing many sses. Joseph made a temporary treaty with the soldiers, trading stock and pplies with them. Howard was close behind Joseph's braves, who were oving from Craig's Mountain to Cottonwood.

#52. Chief Joseph, Orator and Statesman
(Courtesy AZUSA PUBLISHING, LLC)

COTTONWOOD

Captain McConville rode hard from Slate Creek, to reinforce Captain Whipple's command. On July 4th, some supposedly fearful Indians ran from his soldiers near Norton. He didn't take the bait. Joseph was camped two miles north of Cottonwood, positioning warriors on both sides of the road. Captain Whipple had sent Lieutenant Rains' detachment to scout for Joseph's Nez Perce and to report back.

Captain Rains and his men rode right into Joseph's trap and caught in the crossfire, they ran for cover. The ambushed soldiers were massacred. Joseph lost nine braves in the skirmish. As Whipple arrived, on July 4, he knew from a distance that they were too late and placed his men in combat position near the massacre site. The hostiles attacked Whipple and his troops at Cottonwood House. Joseph lost nine warriors.

Captain Perry and his troops waited hours for an attack. Instead, Joseph's warriors attacked the citizens of Mt. Idaho. On July 5th the Indians sent up smoke signals, in three billowy puffs, from a plateau, three miles away. The next day, Randall and Evans tried to break through the hostiles lines, but were killed, McConville arrived too late. Simpson and Whipple and remaining troops rode on to rescue the citizens. Howard did a reversed his order, turned his troops around on a night march, to join Perry in Grangeville by July 9th. Warriors attacked Major Shearer at Mount Idaho, July 9th.

CHIEF LOOKING GLASS

With Howard and his soldiers on the move, many more of Joseph's tribe went back to the reservation or joined Chief Looking Glass on the Clearwater, 4 miles south of Kooskia. Braves had left there to join the hostiles. Getting wind of this, Howard ordered a raid on the camp of Chief Looking Glass.

Captain Whipple and his men rode to the Indian's camp hoping to capture the Nez Perce and take them to Mount Idaho. They reached the camp at dawn. Chief Looking Glass came out to meet them waving a white flag. Whipple asked the chief to surrender, but he refused, as someone began firing on the camp. The Indians returned fire while Looking Glass joined them in their retreat.

Looking Glass's band joined Joseph on the Clearwater River. He addressed the chiefs and vowed to fight the Bluecoats. He had considered going in to the reservation, before. Howard's order to attack him changed his mind. Meanwhile, some of his braves had told Chinese workers that they were going to war on the white man and would make a raid on the Clearwater in 48 hours. Major Shearer sent 20 volunteers to the Clearwater from Mount Idaho.

On July 9, Howard followed Joseph's path of retreat. Joseph had made camp at Horseshoe Bend and prepared to cross the Salmon River. Ollokut and White Bird wanted to cross the Salmon River to outdistance the general. Thesechiefs had the mind-set that if they could escape Howard's jurisdiction, they could make it to Canada. The tribesmen were joined at Horseshoe Bend by Five Wounds, Rainbow, and other Nez Perce warriors who were back from the buffalo hunt. The chief council planned their strategy.

Joseph was a natural born leader and warrior chieftain. In Joseph's retreat, he had led his whole village, beginning with an estimated 750 tribespeople and some 400 mounted warriors into battle. They rode their riding their splendid Appaloosa horses and other breeds that had been bred by the Nez Perce Tribe. Joseph's Nez Perce herded around 2,000 head and pack mules, as they retreated toward Canada. Horse-drawn travois dragged lodge-poles, carrying goods, hides and infants. Some of their horses were lost or stolen in battle; the Nez Perce rounded up and stole more to replenish their stock. Had the warriors made the run to Canada without their families, they could have easily made it to King George's country. Chief White Bird would make it into Canada.

THE CLEARWATER

Thinking they were far ahead of Howard's army, Joseph made camp near Cottonwood Creek on the Clearwater River, where he joined Chief Looking Glass. Horses grazed on the grassy hillsides and the braves fished and hunted to fill their bellies. Young braves raided small farms stealing cattle and horses. The Indians held a powwow, war dance, played stick games and raced their horses On July 11th, army volunteers accidentally surveyed the unsuspecting Indians who were in across the Clearwater River, holding horse races, as part of their festivities. The Battle of the Clearwater ensued. Toohulhutsote led 24 warriors across the river to meet Howard's attack, other braves rushed to join him.

With 400 men and 182 scouts, Howard ordered the attack, as his soldiers dug in and built rock barriers. With Perry and Whipple on their right and left flanks, the hostiles were caught in the middle. They caught one line of soldiers in their crossfire and 400 soldiers rushed to their aid. The Indians met the charge.

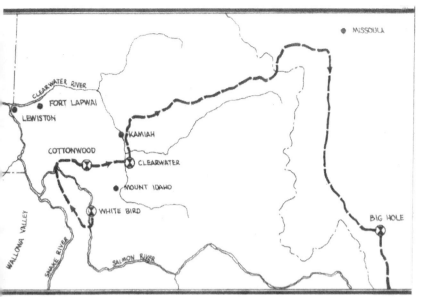

#53. Map of Chief Joseph's Retreat from White Bird Creek in Idaho country to Big Hole, in Montana Territory. (Courtesy of the Idaho State Historical Society Library)

#54. General Howard, Colonel's Miles and Conner plus scenes of the Nez Perce War from Harper's Magazine in 1877. (Courtesy of the Idaho State Historical Society)

Chiefs Joseph and White Bird rode along their lines giving war-cries, encouraging the warriors to fight. Their voices were heard above the din. One warrior appeared on a ridge within rifle range, dancing and waving a red blanket, touting the soldiers. Indians chanted eerie death and scalp chants through the night.

At dawn, as pack-trains arrived, the Nez Perce were quick to attack, killing two soldiers. Indians made sallies on foot and horseback. The fighting was heavy. A cloud of acrid gun-smoke shrouded the field. War-cries and rebel yells continued to fill the air. Company B and the 21st Infantry began firing on each other.

Lieutenant Leary of the 4th Artillery ran between them with his rifle held by two hands in the air, shouting, "Cease fire," ending the melee. Canteens had gone dry. Soldiers were parched. July 12, Miller and Perry made an assault on the spring held by the Indian snipers. They gained control of the spring. Under heavy fighting, the soldiers pushed the Indians back. The braves defended their camp for 30 hours.

Captain Miles arrived with 200 more men and Joseph ordered his people to pack up their goods and teepees. With Miles arrival, Howard then had 600 soldiers to face 100 Nez Perce warriors. He launched a full frontal charge. Crossing the Clearwater River, the Indians fled leaving food cooking and lodges standing. In all Howard realized 13 dead and 23 wounded. Joseph claimed four dead and six wounded. The Nez Perce were outnumbered six to one. Howard had Gatling guns and Howitzers versus Joseph's warriors Winchesters.

On July 13 Howard's Cavalry appeared on the bluffs overlooking Kamiah Valley. They rode down to the water's edge, where the hostiles had completed crossed the treacherous Clearwater River. Joseph's snipers fired on the soldiers across the river. Militia returned fire with Gatling guns and rifles. The snipers scattered the cavalry with their bullets, giving Joseph time to escape.

Joseph broke camp, sending a messenger to Howard asking for terms of surrender. Joseph said that he did not want to leave the land of his forefathers or bring misery on his people. The chiefs then sent No Heart, a Nez Perce warrior under a white flag, to speak with Howard about surrender. He returned to Kamiah after hearing the news of Chief Joseph's wanting for terms for surrender. The messenger, No Heart and his wife also surrendered at that time.

"TRAIL OF TEARS"

The Nez Perce began their ascent up the Lolo Trail over the Bitterroot Mountains. The trek over the Lolo Trail has been referred to as the Nez Perce Trail of Tears, for the hardships and struggles that they faced. On July 16, Joseph met his tribesman, Red Heart, as he was returning home from the "buffalo hunt" on the upper Missouri. He did not join Joseph, but continued on to Lapwai. Howard captured the group and claimed he had taken them prisoner at the Battle of the Clearwater. They stripped the peaceful band of personal belongings, guns and horses, and then marched them to Fort Vancouver; where

ey were held until spring. Joseph held a council on the Weippe Prairie, at the
ginning of the Lolo Trail. Chiefs Looking Glass, Too-hul-hut-sote, and White
rd wanted to join the Crow Indians in "buffalo country." Looking Glass
cided to escape to the land of the Crows and gain their freedom. He was a
eamer. The Crow Indians had long been enemies of the Nez Perce, yet he
ought they were allies. Joseph refused, not wanting to leave "the land of their
thers." It was Old Joseph's wish. The older chiefs opposed Joseph, threatening
s life and again accused him of cowardice. Actually, Joseph was just the
posite. He was established as the true leader to lead the people to Canada. He
ade Pile of Clouds his war-leader. It was decided that messengers would be
nt to chiefs Charlotte and Michel of the Flathead and Pend d' Oreille tribes to
in permission to pass through their country.

Three miles from what is now Orofino, Idaho, fifty warriors formed a
ar guard. A trap had been set. Trees were sawed to drop across the path of
treat. Major Mason almost fell for the ambush, but a rifle shot from
cConville's troops warned them of trouble. One scout was dead, two injured
d two captured.

FORT FIZZLE

As the Nez Perce traveled down Lolo Canyon July 25th, their progress
s impeded by an obstruction built by Captain Charles C. Rawn and 44
ldiers. A bulwark, named Fort Fizzle, blocked the trail to the Bitterroot
alley. Rawn recruited about 100 settlers and 30 additional soldiers to guard
ainst Indians. The structure was three feet high. A rifle trench was dug. Rawn
ld a council with Joseph, White Bird and Looking Glass.

The next day Captain Rawn heard them singing, high on a ridge along
e side of the cliff. They moved in single file along the trail high above. The
dians mused at having fooled Rawn and proceeded toward the Bitterroots.
ere, they bought coffee, flour, sugar and tobacco from merchants. In
evensville one merchant wouldn't sell to the Indians, but other shop owners
ofited. The Indians used money for their purchases. They crossed Lolo Creek
d ventured up a grade onto Weippe Prairie, with water and grass.

Some braves returned to Kamiah following Major Mason for days as he
oved toward Missoula. These braves had burned homes in Kamiah and stolen
estock. Joseph's cavalry began rounding up their strays and stole ponies from
aceful Indians in the valley acquiring a herd of some 700 horses. Howard was
layed eight days waiting for to arrive from Fort Boise. He assigned Major
hn Green and complement from Fort Boise to guard the Camas Prairie. He
dered more troops from Georgia and Washington Territory. Howard's personal
mmand

#55. War-chief Joseph
(Courtesy Azusa Publishing LLC)

consisted of Captain Miller's 21st Infantry, captained by Captain Evan Miles and a battalion of four companies of the first cavalry, under Major George Sanford, Howard rested at Kamiah before continuing in pursuit of the hostiles. He left half of his troops to pursue Joseph. The ascent above Kamiah with wagons and heavy guns was rugged with slippery trails, undergrowth, rocks and fallen timber, a 16 mile trek to Weippe Prairie. Howard constantly recruited troops for battle and outnumbering Joseph's forces. Yet, Joseph fought brilliantly throughout the whole campaign and was only reinforced one time, by Looking Glass.

BIG HOLE

Chief Joseph's warriors were beginning to tire as they reached Big Hole. Making camp there, Pile of Clouds their Medicine Man, had a bad feeling, saying death was on their trail, but they did not heed his warning. They held a feast, as was their tradition, while some braves went out and hunted antelope. They played stick games, sang and did a war dance. Unsuspecting, the Nez Perce slept in their lodges when the soldiers arrived. After nightfall General Gibbon moved into position. At dawn, on August 9th, one lone Indian rider rode out to check the horses. A bullet dropped him from the saddle, awakening the camp. A war-whoop followed, waking anyone that had been asleep. Warriors ran for cover. Gibbon's men completely surrounded them. In previous battles, the warriors' families had been isolated, away from the fighting. This assault was a bloody massacre, as soldiers shot or clubbed any Indians that moved in their blankets with rifle butts. The Big Hole encampment was Looking Glass' responsibility. Relieved of duty, Leaning Elk assumed his duties.

Believing that they had won the fight, the soldiers began to burn the lodges, but White Bird's warriors drove them back. Joseph ordered them to break camp and load the pack-horses. His warriors captured Gibbon's canon and ammunition, disabling the howitzer. They left and let it lay. The braves started a fire that raged toward the soldiers, fueled by strong wind, but it changed directions and died out. By evening 29 soldiers were dead, including Gen. Gibbon and 40 injured. As General Howard arrived the Indians disappeared. Joseph lost 12, including women and children, along with his two wives dead. Looking Glasses' daughter and some of his best warriors, including Rainbow and Five Wounds were killed. Ironically, Walaitits and Red Moccasin Tops, died there. After burying his dead, Joseph continued his flight. He rallied his braves out of the fray to a position on higher ground. They caught a number of stray ponies. The Indians departed Big Hole Basin, crossing back into what is now Idaho. and Lemhi Canyon. Chief White Bird held council with the Shoshoni and attempted to gain their support against General Howard. Mostly enemies of the Nez Perce, the Shoshoni refused the offer. Howard received word

#56. Joseph rests in solitude.
(Courtesy of Idaho State Historical Society)

that they were raiding ranches and leaving the carcasses of cattle they had slaughtered as they lay. The Nez Perce massacred eight men on a ranch at Horse Prairie Creek. Chief White Bird was blamed for the attack. The braves involved had found a keg of whiskey, which led to their actions. They headed for Yellowstone. Howard tried to cut them off, and sent Lt. George Bacon and forty men to intercept them at Targhee (Tah-gee) Pass. Captains Calloway and Norton arrived from Virginia City to reinforce Howard's column.

August 17th, after the Big Hole Massacre, the Nez Perce held council, deciding to raid Howard's camp for horses on. The general's men were tuckered so he pushed to reach Camas Meadows where they could camp and rest. They felt secure with a heavy guard posted. Two Nez Perce had been seen milling around, but nothing was thought of it. Joseph's spies watched their every move. One hundred fifty soldiers set up camp and retired, thinking the Indians were far away. Joseph's scouts apprised him of Howard's position. As it became dark, 40 Nez Perce warriors slipped silently into camp. The sentry thought they were soldiers. The warriors cut loose the mules, before they were discovered and remained silent. The sentry discharged his weapon, awakening the camp.

War-cries broke the silence, as the braves stampeded nearly 150 mules, by waving buffalo robes. The attack caused confusion, as the soldiers clamored to dress and find their guns. A bugler blew the call to attack. The Indians drew fire as they rode out. Howard ordered his officers to recapture the mules. Captains Carr, Jackson, and Norton took chase after the fleeting renegades, who had gained distance. Carr led the attack. Jackson and Norton joined Carr in rapid-fire, the Indians returned fire. Joseph stationed snipers surrounding the cavalry, pinning them down. The bugler blew retreat as the troops under the heavy cross-fire withdrew. Lieutenant Benson received a bullet through his buttocks. Carr recaptured the mules, but lost them again. Chief Joseph's double-flank movement succeeded. His warriors picked off soldiers who were trying to reach their horses, some 500 yards away. It took Howard's full complement to rescue Norton.

YELLOWSTONE

Seeing General Howard, the Indians retreated. Howard then pursued the hostiles, who now had a three day lead. Chief Joseph continued along the LoLo Trail, against the Rockies, toward Yellowstone. W. T. Sherman, General of the Army, had been in Yellowstone Park during a tour of the western forts. He was escorted by Lieutenant Colonel Gilbert and two cavalry troops from Fort Benton. General Sherman left the park shortly before the Nez Perce hostiles passed through.

#57. Joseph with his Famous Rifle-
(Courtesy of Idaho State Historical Society)

As the fugitives passed through Yellowstone, they encountered the ɔwan party, tourists from Helena. The Indians broke up their wagon, stealing mp equipment and supplies. Although his chiefs wanted to free the tourists ıruly braves shot Cowan and let his body lay. Other tourists left Helena for ɛllowstone Park. Renegades shot a Mr. Weikert as he rode his horse. The ɔunt stumbled, throwing him, but still holding his pistol; he jumped to his feet d fired at the warriors. He remounted, still firing at the braves who were ınning toward him. Others pillaged the camp, stealing horses and gear. They ırned everything remaining. The warriors killed Mr. Kenk, stole from Mr. ɛwart, but spared his life. Others made it to Mammoth Springs. Two survivors ntinued on to Virginia City.

General Howard was never under manned. He had scouts and curriers ıo kept him informed and used the telegraph to track Joseph's position and ɔvements. Military companies dispatched from around the country were nstantly coming to join the fray keeping his numbers of fighting men up, ɔward was never overpowered and he sent a currier to General Sturgis structing him to travel at top speed along the Yellowstone River in an attempt detain Joseph's Nez Perce, but the message arrived too late. Meantime, the ɛz Perce killed two mountain men and a boy that Sturgis had deployed to ʳvey the Indians' position.

The trail of the renegades was discovered along the Stinking Water ver. Looking Glass had ridden ahead to council with the Crow Indians, but ɛy chose neutrality. A scout told Chief Joseph that Sturgis was ahead and that ɛ prairie was on fire. The Indians continued on toward Canada. The Nez Perce w numbered 400 warriors strong. Joseph sent a group of his braves toward ırt Mountain, dragging bundles of brush behind their horses, hiding their ɔks. Sturgis led the 7th cavalry after them, post haste. When General Sturgis ɔcated, he left a clearing large enough for the Indians to travel through, as seph had planned. He eluded both Howard and Sturgis at Clark's Fork. Sturgis d been tricked. The officers met and decided that Lieutenant Otis, with 50 ɛn, cannons and mules would pursue them.

BATTLE OF CANYON CREEK

Colonial Sturgis intercepted him at Canyon Creek, by traveling west ɔng the Yellowstone River and the Battle of Canyon Creek ensued. Canyon ɛek was a dry wash surrounded by 10 to 20 foot walls. On September 13th, ɛ hostiles began firing on them from both sides of the canyon. Sturgis drove ɛ Indians back. The braves fought hard to regain ground. Sturgis ordered nteen to lead his cavalry around the hills, cross the creek to try and cut off the ʳse herd. He ordered Merrill to protect Benteen's flank.

As the cavalry rode out the Indians anticipated their move, peppering ɛm with bullets. The soldiers had to dismount. Lieutenant Otis advanced on ɔt with his "Jackass Battery." The Nez Perce drove them back. Sturgis' plan had backfired. Captain French's Company M gave boisterous yells, as th[e] rushed up the hillside in an effort to reach the Indians. Some were mounte[d] while others walked. Seeing warriors in a group, soldiers fired directly on the[m] killing some. The Seventh advanced onto the valley floor and were met with barrage of Indians' bullets. The sniper fire pinned them down. Joseph had he[ld] Sturgis. The soldiers made camp, being exhausted. During the night, Josep[h] Nez Perce broke camp and continued their retreat. With the army's use howitzers, 21 Nez Perce had died, while the army lost 3 with 11 wounded.

The next day, Joseph's people entered the "land of the Crows." Inste[ad] of the nirvana Chief Looking Glass anticipated, it became a fight with their o[ld] enemies, the Crow Indians. A running battle began that stretched over 1[2] miles. The Nez Perce lost nearly 900 spent horses. The Crows fought them within 40 miles of the Musselshell River, before retreating.

The Nez Perce braves commandeered a stagecoach, burned the w[ay] station buildings and took turns driving the coach until they got bored. Th[ey] then destroyed it and burned the mail. The driver and passengers had escap[ed] into the brush and were rescued by Howard. The Nez Perce outdistanc[ed] Sturgis, traveling along the Musselshell River. Joseph made a wide sweep w[est] around the Judith Mountains.

COW ISLAND

On September 23th they reached the freight depot on Cow Island. Ch[ief] Joseph's braves crossed the Missouri River and attacked the garrison, which w[as] sheltered by a small earthwork structure, guarded by Sergeant Willia[m] Mulchert, twelve soldiers of the Seventh Cavalry and four citizens, w[ho] defended over 50 tons of supplies. The goods had just been unloaded from t[he] Steamship Benton onto the bank of the river.

The steamer had departed down the Missouri before the Nez Perce ra[id]. Joseph offered to surrender in exchange for 200 bags of sugar, but was refuse[d]. They then stole the sugar and took the supplies that they wanted, burning t[he] rest. The "Skirmish at Cow Island" lasted 18 hours, two volunteers we[re] wounded.

Major Ilges and 36 volunteers left Fort Benton for Cow Island September 25th and began tracking the hostiles up Cow Creek Canyo[n]. Lieutenant Hardin brought soldiers down river by boat. After ten miles a sc[out] located the Indian encampment. The combatants had surrounded a wagon-tra[in] near Judith Basin. As the soldiers arrived the Indians were setting fire to t[he] wagons. Seven emigrants fled into the hills. The Nez Perce rode down t[he] canyon for about half a mile and attacked the troops. Shortly, the warri[ors] disappeared. The major and his men had taken cover and from the high grou[nd] the Indians initiated gunfire.

The fracas started about noon and for two hours they fought. They we[re] terribly accurate with their rifles without showing themselves. They ceas[ed] firing from the front. Major Ilges suspected a rear offensive and retreated

Cow Island. Snipers held them down until the Nez Perce had escaped. One citizen and a horse were killed and two Indians injured. Chief Joseph anticipated no one opposition in buffalo country. Miles shelled the bluff and signaled the Steamship Benton to return to Cow Island Crossing.

MILK RIVER

The end of September, 1877 the Nez Perce camped along the Milk River where there was plenty of drinking water and firewood. The tribe had ample time to rest. Their horses grazed to gain back some of the weight lost from constantly being on the move and in battle. Man and horse were exhausted from the endless fighting. The Nez Perce had plenty of antelope, buffalo, and deer to provide their meat and winter robes. They could relax with General Howard far behind them. They built up their winter stores, rested and tended their wounds.

They then continued on reaching the vicinity of the Bear Paw Mountains 1300 miles from Wallowa Valley and just 40 miles from the Canadian border. Rain mixed with snow as the tribe faced the task of the last leg of their journey into Canada. Joseph and his twelve year old daughter readied their horses and adjusted the loads, anticipating their quest.

Out of nowhere, rode a line of cavalrymen charging the camp. Fifty or sixty braves were guarding the horses. Colonel Miles had the advantage, with 500 cavalrymen, infantry, and Cheyenne Indian scouts. His complement was equipped with a breech-loading Hotchkiss gun and a twelve pound Napoleon cannon. Miles used a double line of the 2nd and 7th Cavalry in an attempt to divide and conquer in a single charge.

Joseph and his daughter were cut off from the camp. He gave her a rope and told her to tether the horses, before joining the others that were isolated. Joseph broke and ran through the melee. Reaching his lodge, his wife handed Joseph his rifle saying, "go and fight."

Miles' column caught Joseph, splitting his ranks. Joseph's brother, Ollokut was killed. Joseph rushed to his family and though greatly outnumbered, the Nez Perce pushed the soldiers back, but Miles held his ground. The Cavalry stampeded the Indians' horses, but Miles had lost 26 men. 40 were wounded. Joseph's losses were 18 men and three women. It had been a costly battle. Joseph had just lost two wives at Big Hole. Now his brother, Ollokut was dead, as was Chief Looking Glass.

#58. Chief Joseph stands in front of his
teepee, at home in Lapwai.
(Courtesy of Charles Winters)

SURRENDER

An interesting antidote is that Chief White Bird and 103 men, 60 women and 8 children actually made it into Canada, during the fighting in the Bear Paw Mountains. He escorted over one third of the non-treaty Nez Perce across the Bear Paw Mountains into Canada. Sioux Chief Sitting Bull, who was exiled there, received White Bird and his band in peace. The Nez Perce were finally free. They took up residence, there. Some returned to Idaho much later over time, but Nez Perce Indians still reside in the foothills of the Canadian Rockies.

Joseph stated that if they had left the women, children and injured; they could have left the country. His flight for freedom to King George's land had failed. Joseph lastly sent Yellow Bull to talk with Colonel Miles, who demanded surrender, assuring safe passage. Miles promised that if Joseph surrendered the Nez Perce could go back home. Yellow Bull wondered if Colonel Miles was sincere. Cheyenne scouts spoke with Joseph and told him they believed Miles truly wanted peace. Miles gave Joseph no definite answer. The fifth day of talks, on October 5, 1877 War Chief Joseph surrendered, giving up his rifle. He uttered those famous words:

"Hear me my chiefs, I am tired. My heart is sick and sad. From where the sun now stands, I will fight no more, forever."

Never-the-less Joseph and Miles always remained friends. Colonel Miles and his troops escorted Joseph and his people to Tongue River but they were taken to Bismarck, against Miles' wishes. They were then ordered to Leavenworth and forced to live by a river that was unclean. They bathed, drank and cooked from that river, resulting in many deaths. From there they were shipped by rail to Baxter, in Kansas Territory. Three died in the box-cars. Seventy Nez Perce died of exposure.

Joseph told officials of Miles' promise to return them to Wallowa but it was not kept. He and 150 Nez Perce were exiled in Indian Territory in Oklahoma, and then shipped by rail to the Colville Reservation. Joseph never saw his Wallowa Valley again. Broken hearted, Joseph died before his teepee fire September 21, 1904.

During his retreat, Chief Joseph became a famous folk hero in the American Northwest. He is still one of the most popular American Indians. He earned the respect of the Army officers who fought him, remaining close friends with General Miles, for the rest of his life. Miles had received a promotion to general over the Army. Joseph met and befriended Buffalo Bill Cody. Joseph traveled to Washington D.C. in 1897, to meet with President William McKinley. Chief Joseph's bust appeared on a postage stamp in 1972 and 2003.

#59. Chief Joseph at surrender in the Bear Paws
(Courtesy of AZUSA PUBLISHING, LLC)

THE NEZ PERCE RESERVATION

The Nez Perce Indian Reservation is on the Columbia River Plateau, cated in Idaho, Oregon and Washington, including the Clearwater, Salmon and ake Rivers. The population for the reservation was 17,959 tribes-people in the ar 2,000. The Nez Perce Tribe has an Appaloosa horse breeding program. shers in the tribe are active in tribal fisheries on the Columbia River, between nneville and McNary Dams. They also fish for Chinook salmon and steelhead ring the spring and summer runs. The Nez Perce Tribe operates a fish tchery on the Clearwater River and other hatcheries. The largest town on the servation is Orofino, in northeastern Idaho. The reservation headquarters is at pwai, Idaho. Other towns on the reservation include Ahsahka, Craigmont, ldesac and Ferdinand.

NEZ PERCE MYTHOLOGY

Long ago, seven giant brothers lived in the Blue Mountains. The giant nsters were taller than the tallest pine trees and strongest oaks. The ancient es hated the monsters because they ate children. The tribal headmen said that one in the tribe could beat them. The headman went to Coyote for help. yote agreed to help, but knew that he could not beat the seven monsters. yote went to friend fox. Fox said to dig seven deep holes. Coyote called all of animals with sharp claws to dig. He called beaver, bears, cougars, marmots, ce and rats to dig. They dug seven deep holes. Coyote filled them with a ddish yellow liquid. Hot rocks from the fires were then placed in the liquid. en the giants moved through to the east, they dropped into the boiling pits. yote told the monsters that they would be punished for their evil deeds. They uggled and roared in pain. Coyote told them that they would be turned into l mountains. He jumped out from his hiding place and turned them into tall untains and made a very deep gorge in front of them. Coyote struck the earth, ening a deep gorge, now known as Hell's Canyon and the Snake River.

CHIEF JOSEPH'S, LEGEND OF THE LAKE

Many moons ago the Nez Perce tribe was strong. Every summer the rriors rode to the Upper Missouri into buffalo country to hunt. One such mmer, Red Wolf of the Nez Perce Indians and his band were attacked by ackfoot warriors. They held their ground and on their buffalo hunt the next mmer, they were again attacked by the Blackfeet. On this occasion they took ackfoot scalps. Then, the Blackfeet attacked them at night and killed many. d Wolf and his band fought the Blackfeet on the run. Finally enemy stopped to camp because it was too dark to see. They camped by a e, built a huge bonfire, and danced around it.

In the Nez Perce camp, the women wailed for the dead. There was no ncing, only sorrow. Their campfires were out. Young Chief Red Wolf had only

one daughter. She was the beautiful Indian princess, Wahluna. She knew th
her father and his warriors were too weak to fight again. She took a canoe a
paddled across the lake. She emerged in the firelight of the lodge of a t
warrior and spoke to him and told him that she was Wahluna the daughter
Nez Perce Chief Red Wolf and that she had come to speak to the great chief
the Blackfeet. He told her that he was Blackfeet Bloody Chief and asked h
what she had to say to him.

I have come to plead for my people. Our women are wailing for the
fallen warriors and we have no fires in our camp. My father said you will co
and kill us tomorrow. I know you do not want the scalps of women and childre
We can never fight Bloody Chief, again. Our warriors are dead. Wahluna lay
the sand and covered her face. Bloody Chief (Tlesca) covered her shoulde
with his robe and told Wahluna that she was brave and that she loved h
people. His heart grieved for her. He told her he would never fight her peop
again. The young warrior's words angered his father. He told Tlesca to pick
his robe and kill the girl. He said her people were dogs. Red Wolf is no do
When he staggered, Red Wolf still fought bravely. I was strong enough to fig
him. He broke my shoulder with his war club. I will leave my robe on h
shoulders. Bloody Chiefs heart softened. He loved his son. He too, put his ro
around the girl. Tlesca said that the girl was brave and beautiful. He said that
twelve moons an owl would hoot down by the lake.

Wahluna returned to her village. Her people were not attacked a
could again build their campfires. On the twelfth moon, she listened for the o
hooting. She slipped through the village and down to the lake. Wahluna n
Tlesca there. He told her that some Blackfoot girls had eyed him, but his hea
was with her. Wahluna told him that it could not be, that her people would fe
his bones to the wolves.

Tlesca told her that when six more moons came, to listen for the ho
of the gray wolf. Again, Wahluna returned to her village. She waited anxious
for six more moons. She paddled her canoe across the lake and met Tlesca.
informed her that he had talked with his father and that they would come to R
Wolf's village the next morning. We smoke the peace pipe. We fish in your la
You hunt the buffalo in peace.

The next day Bloody Chief and his sub-chiefs all came to Red Wo
village and smoked the pipe of peace. Bloody Chief and Red Wolf agreed th
Tlesca and Wahluna could marry. Red Wolf sent runners to the Nez Per
people along the Kooskia and to his friends among the Cayuse and Yakima.
invited them to a great wedding feast. At sunrise the day of the wedding fea
Tlesca and Wahluna went out on the lake in a canoe. Suddenly, the wa
stirred. Tlesca and Wahluna headed toward shore. Waves rose high in the a
The head of a serpent appeared out of the depths. It rose out of the water.
swam around and struck the boat with its mighty tail. The serpent disappeare
The young couple was never seen again.

#60. Joseph As he was illustrated on the
United States postage stamp.
(Courtesy of the U.S. Postal Service)

INDEX

Bibliography

Adams, Glen, The Coeur d'Alene Indian Reservation, Fairfield, Ye Galleon Press, 1999

Addison, Helen and McGrath, Dan L. Lincoln, Nebraska, Third Bison Book Printing, 1967

Aswell, Reg, Indian Tribes, Seattle, Hancock House Publishers, Ltd., 1978

Baker, Paul E., The Forgotten Kutenai, Mountain States Press, Boise, 1955

Beal, Merrill D., "I Will Fight No More Forever," New York, Ballantine Books, 1971

Bird, Laurie Annie, Old Fort Boise, Caldwell, Idaho, Caxton Printers, Ltd., 1990

Bolen, Robert D., "Smoke Signals & Wagon Tracks," Nampa, Idaho, Fort Boise Publishing Company, 2009

Butler, Robert, B., A Guide to Understanding Idaho Archeology (Third Edition) The Upper Snake and Salmon River

Clark, Ella E., Indian Legends of the Pacific Northwest, Berkley and Los Angeles, U of C Press, 1953.Convis, Charles L., Native American Women, Carson City, Pioneer Press, 1996

Corless, Hank, The Weiser Indians, Salt Lake, University of Utah Press, 1990

Dary, David, The Oregon Trail, an American Saga, New York, Oxford University Press, 2004

Derig, Betty, Roadside History of Idaho, Missoula, Mt., Mountain Press Publishing Company, 199

Evancho, Joe, Fishing Idaho, Boise, Cutthroat Press, 2,004

Fahey, John, The Kalispel Indians, Norman, University of Oklahoma Press, 1986

Johnson, Michael, The Native Tribes of America, London, Compendium Publishing, 1999

Hailey, John, History of Idaho, Boise, Syms-York, 1910

Kloss, Doris, Sarah Winnemucca, Minneapolis, Dillon Press, 1986

Kootenai Culture Committee & Confederated Salish and Kootenai Tribes, How Marten Got His Spots and other Kootenai Indian Stories, Helena, Montana Historical Society Press & Salish Kootenai College Press, 2,000

Howard, Helen Addison & McGrath, Dan L., War Chief Joseph, Caldwell, Idaho, Caxton Printers, Ltd. 1967

Kootenai Culture Committee & Confederated Salish and Kootenai Tribes, Owl's Eyes & Seeking Spirit, Helena, Montana Historical Society Press & Salish Kootenai College Press, 1981

Lappert, Dorothy, PhD & Spignesi, Stephen J., Native History for Dummies, Hoboken, 2998

Madsen, Brigham D., Chief Pocatello, Moscow, University of Idaho Press, 1999

Madsen, Brigham D., The Bannocks, Moscow, University of Idaho Press, 1996

Madsen, Brigham D., The Northern Shoshone, Caldwell, Idaho, Caxton Printers, Ltd. 1980

Members of the Potomac Corral, Great Western Indian Fights, Lincoln, Nebraska, Bison Books, 1966

Miller, Rod, Massacre at Bear River, Caldwell, Idaho, Caxton Printers, Ltd., 1952

Painter, Bob, White Bird, Fairfield, Washington, Ye Galleon Press, 2002

Salisbury, Albert & Jane, Lewis & Clark, the Journey West, New York, Promontory Press, 1990

Salish Pend d' Oreille Culture Committee CSKT, The Salish People and the Lewis and Clark Expedition, Norman, University of Oklahoma Press, 1966

Stein, Julie K. Exploring Coast Salish Prehistory, Seattle University of Washington Press, 2000

Shannon, Donald H., The Boise Massacre on the Oregon Trail, Caldwell, Idaho, Snake River Publishers, 2004.

Steward, Julian H. Plateau Aboriginal Sociopolitical Groups, Salt Lake, University of Utah Press, 1970.

Walker Jr., Deward E., Indians of Idaho, Moscow, University Press of Idaho, 1982.

Citing Electronic Publications

<http:www.accessgeneology.com/native/tribes,kutenai/kutenaiindiantribe.htm>
<http:www.anglerguide.com/articles/18c.html>
<http:www.answere.com/topic/paiute>
<http:www.bigfootforums.com/lofiversion/index.php/tii5.68.html>
<http:www.clarkontheyellowstone.org/sig_event.html>
<http:www.geocities.com/naforts/id.html>
<http:www.historynet.com/Utah-war-us-government-versus-mormon-settlers.htm>
<http:www.home.att.net/~mman/DoriansWife.htm>
<http:www.kstrom.net/isk/maps/Dakotas/sd.html>
<http:www.legendsofAmerica.com/id-forthall.html>
<http:www.Mountainmeadowsmassacre.com/>
<http:www.mnh.si.edu/lewisandclark/resources/Camissa.pdf>
<http://www.narhist.ewu.edu/Native_Americans/timelines/timeline_wars_treaties.html>
<http:www.newadvent.org/cathen/04093a.htm>
<http:www. newadvent.org/cathen/08594a.htm>
<http:www. newadvent.org/cathen/08711a.htm>
<http:www.newworldencyclopedia.org/entry/Shoshone>
<accesshttp:www.newworldencyclopedia.org/entryConfederated_Salish_andKootenai_Tribes_..>
<http:www.nps.gov/archive/fola/Laramie.htm>
<http:www. parksandrecreation.idaho.gov/parks/oldmission.aspx>
<http:www.primitiveways.com/tule_ethnobotany.html>
<http:www.reference.com/browse/Northern%20Paiute>
<http:www.rootsweb.ancestry.com/~idbounda/kutenais.htm
<http:www.rootsweb.ancestry.com/~idreserv/cdhist.html>
<http:www.rootsweb.ancestry.com/~idreserv/>
<http:www.shoshonebannocktribes.com>
<http://www.suite 101.com/article.cfm/old_west/911817>
<http:www.washingtonwars.net/Ward%20Massacre.htm>
<http:tripcheck.com/poses/SBhellcanyon.asp>
<http:www.windriverhistory.org/exhibits/chiefjoseph/chiefjosephupdate6805.pdf>

The Author explores inside of a 19th Century stone house in southeastern Oregon.

About the Author

Born in Lexington, Nebraska, Robert Bolen, B.A. has a degree in Archeology/Anthropology. In Archeology class he was informed that because of his features, the Mongolian Eye-fold, that he was part Indian. In 1755 a Bolen ancestor was taken captive by Delaware Indians. She was later rescued with her baby daughter, Robb's Great, Great, Grandmother. At the time of rescue, the poor girl (just 17) was scalped, but lived. The French scalp was the size of a silver dollar. Family says that she combed her hair hiding the scar and managed to live to be over one hundred years of age. Bolen' served under George Washington in the American Revolution. In 1777 the author's ancestors erected Fort Bolin near Cross Creek, Pennsylvania for protection from Indian attacks. Two ancestors were killed in Kentucky by Shawnee Indians allied to the British. Great Granddad Gilbert Bolen rode with the Ohio Fourth Cavalry in the Civil War under General Sherman; in 1866, he brought his wife and six children west to Nebraska in a Conestoga wagon. Grand-dad Denver Colorado Bolen knew Buffalo Bill Cody in western Nebraska. Bolen is an authority on Indian artifacts and trade beads. Robb and Dori Bolen reside in Nampa, near Boise, Idaho. Robb owns the website, Fort Boise Bead Trader.

PHOTOGRAPHS COURTESY OF AZUSA Publishing, LLC

3575 S. Fox Street
Englewood, CO 80110

Email: azusa@azusapublishing.com

Phone Toll-free: 888-783-0077

Phone/Fax: 303-783-0073

Email: azusa@azusapublishing.com

Mailing address: P.O. Box 2526, Englewood, CO 80150

CPSIA information can be obtained at www.ICGtesting.com
Printed in the USA
BVOW070401220512

290313BV00005B/1/P